Advance Praise for
Celebrating the Wrath of God

"Jim McGuiggan's provocative ideas will open doors in your mind and heart—as they have in mine—to reconsidering exactly who this God is we claim to worship and what He is up to. *Celebrating the Wrath of God* tackles with realism, wisdom, and a no-punches-pulled writing style a topic important to every honest person. Prepare to access the center of your soul and have whatever's there nudged aside in favor of worship."

—DR. LARRY CRABB, founder of New Way Ministries
and author of *Shattered Dreams*

"Jim McGuiggan applies the lordship of God to suffering and pain, and the author is one who knows that reality personally. In *Celebrating the Wrath of God*, I hear the pain of the sufferer, but also the voice of confidence. McGuiggan...reminds us that God is a loving Sovereign who uses the fallen world to unrelenting pursue his people in love."

—JOHN MARK HICKS, professor of theology
at Lipscomb University and author of *Yet Will I Trust Him*

"If you pick up this book you may have difficulty putting it down. Jim McGuiggan combines strong thought with delightful style and speaks to the human condition."

—HADDON ROBINSON, PH.D., co-host and teacher
of Discover the Word radio program and co-director of the
Doctor of Ministry Program at Gordon-Conwell Theological Seminary

"This collection of essays will be a rewarding study for all who are serious about their Christian journey. McGuiggan will push readers to a depth of discussion for which they long and will enable them to recognize that God sees in a way we cannot see. Like a tender-hearted Job who refuses to "push God outside the door" lest God receive "bad press," McGuiggan assumes God's terrible and loving presence to make sense of our existence."

—DAVID FLEER, professor of religion and communication, Rochester College, and co-author of *Preaching Luke/Acts and Preaching Autobiography: Connecting the World of the Preacher and the World of the Text*

Reflections on the Agony and the Ecstasy

of His Relentless Love

CELEBRATING

THE

WRATH

OF GOD

JIM McGUIGGAN

WATERBROOK
PRESS

CELEBRATING THE WRATH OF GOD
PUBLISHED BY WATERBROOK PRESS
2375 Telstar Drive, Suite 160
Colorado Springs, Colorado 80920
A division of Random House, Inc.

ISBN 1-57856-408-5

Library of Congress Cataloging-in-Publication Data
McGuiggan, Jim, 1937–
    Celebrating the wrath of God : reflections on the agony and the ecstasy of his relentless love / by Jim McGuiggan.— 1st ed.
        p. cm.
    Includes bibliographical references.
    ISBN-13: 978-1-578-56408-8
    1. Suffering—Religious aspects—Christianity.   I. Title.

BV4909 .M39 2001
231'.6—dc21

2001017945

Printed in the United States of America
2001—First Edition

146635165

In praise of God,
who shows his power and lovingkindness
in the salvation of entire families:

The Browns of Midland, Texas
The Ledbetters of Fort Lauderdale, Florida
The Rushings of Miami, Florida

In praise of God and glad remembrance of
Mary Chandler's
triumphant life and death.

Contents

INTRODUCTION

The poet W. M. Clow has it right:

> *God loves to be longed for, he longs to be sought,*
> *For he sought us himself with such longing and love,*
> *He died for desire of us, marvelous thought!*
> *And he longs for us now to be with him above.*[1]

His little book repeats the astonishing claim that God adores his creation and longs with an unceasing hunger to live with us in holy friendship as our Lord.

Many people reject this claim as nonsense. We live on a planetary Alcatraz, they tell us, a desolate wasteland. They believe that if there was a God who adored us, he wouldn't allow us to live this way, generation after generation after generation.

Mind you, I'm not just talking about people who are atheists or agnostics. Many Christians are hiding lives of desperation behind masks that say they're coping well, when, in fact, they're struggling and losing against evil forces in their lives. They're fighting patterns of failure that horrify them with strength and durability. They've prayed, begged God for deliverance, and like the poor, bleeding woman in the Gospels, they've gone to all the "doctors" and find themselves no better off. They've spent all they have, and now they're listless, drained. Some parts of their lives are in shambles, and this affects other areas.

The desert they live in seems to have no boundaries. Speechless with grief, they wonder where God is.

Their despondency makes sense. These people don't lie around in recliners with cold beers in their hands, critics of all they survey, enjoying verbal tussles that keep them from coming into contact with real life. No, they're pain-wracked, brokenhearted people who are irritated beyond measure by glib explanations for their suffering. Their deep heartache and struggle is a holy place; we should enter only in a respectful and humble manner, leaving our plodding, overly technical books or slick seven-step cures at home.

This book isn't an exercise in Christian apologetics; it's simply an exposition and proclamation that God is Lord of this wilderness we call life. The only answer to the question of suffering is God. He knows very well about the world's awful wrongs and its inexpressible pain. In the end, it's God's character and his commitment to us that brings us assurance if assurance is to be had.

In every generation, God has been able to persuade millions of people who've been made skeptical through disappointment and loss that he's working a wondrous work that'll leave them speechless with joy when he finally brings them through to glory. They've come to trust in him and know they'll find him not only faithful but capable.

If you're able to give God a brave hearing, the agony of your own life and the vast agony of the world you care about will be easier to live with, easier to make sense of, easier to be hopeful about. He comes to all of us saying, "Give me a chance, let me enter your life, don't give up on me. Before you and I are done, I'll convince you that all you fear and hate and run from will bring to you an eternal weight of glory. When it's over you'll say, 'I wish I could do it again, I'd do it better. I'd live more nobly and trustingly in the wilderness. I'd watch for the signs along the way of God's hand at work. I'd be more assured and more at peace during my struggles.'"

But it isn't only those who hurt who need help. There are those of us whose life is as tame as last week's bus schedule. We suffer no pain, aren't lonely, our family's in good shape, and life is a breeze, and yet…and yet…we sense a profound emptiness. At the beginning of our Christian life, we heard the call of God like a trumpet. Our eyes lit up, we threw ourselves heartfirst into the battle, only later to settle for church attendance, happy songs, and interchurch rivalry. Life is fine, and we can relax because we're no longer in jeopardy.

A mind-set like that's a killer. Gone is any sense of conflict with dark powers. Gone is the conviction that somehow we're fighting God's fight for him against all the forces of cynicism and oppression. Gone is the conviction that what we do in this life makes a difference at the cosmic level. Gone, too, is the sense that daily faithfulness is important to God's galactic purpose.

Let's not lose our place in the biblical story of which we're a part. As believers we are the colony of heaven, fighting our way through a wilderness world with a glad message of galvanizing truth: The wilderness isn't forever. The holy God who made us all has given up on none of us.

Weekly platitudes and assurances that God is a "heavenly sweetheart" who exists to see that his followers don't get hurt or hungry or disturbed—they have their price. For some, they'll do just fine, but for others, there's a restlessness, a feeling of disappointment—"This is it? This? This is what the biblical heroes in Israel and other nations went through purgatory for? This is what Paul had in mind when he talked about tearing down strongholds and taking captive everything that sets itself against God?[2] This is what Paul ran halfway across the world to tell—taking beatings and scourgings as he went, enduring loneliness and betrayal, hunger and slander? All that so we can sit and sing happy songs while humanity goes down into oblivion? This is what Christ died for?"

We know in our bones that that isn't true! His Word tells us Christ died to redeem us and to make right the suffering and sin in the world—in the end. We were made for war as well as peace. We've been sent into the world by Christ, as Christ was sent into the world by his Father. But the suffering and pain of this world's curse falls on everyone, including Christians.

This book claims: God's people are people of the wilderness for the world's sake. We suffer vicariously for the world's sake. This book declares that God's glory is seen with startling clarity in a chaotic world; our vision of God is purified and enriched by wilderness conditions, and many have borne witness to this truth by living honorably and courageously in the midst of the wilderness.

It wasn't until Ezekiel was a captive in Babylon ("the wilderness of the nations"—Ezekiel 20:35, NLT) that the heavens were opened to him (Ezekiel 1:1). Luke tells us:

> In the fifteenth year of the reign of Tiberius Caesar—
> when Pontius Pilate was governor of Judea, Herod
> tetrarch of Galilee, his brother Philip tetrarch of Iturea
> and Trachonitis, and Lysanias tetrarch of Abilene—
> during the high priesthood of Annas and Caiaphas,

the word of God came to John son of Zechariah in the desert. (3:1-2)

While all the noise and clamor was going on in the big cities, while the world's powerbrokers were jockeying for position and reputation in the places of commerce and religion, the word of God was breaking into the world *in the desert!* "Head for the big cities," someone was sure to be advising aspiring young rabbis or politicians. "That's where it's all happening! You've got to be in Jerusalem or Caesarea or you're going nowhere." But the glory of God wasn't seen in the big cities, at the big conferences, in the presence of the major players—it was seen in the wilderness.

Nothing's changed!

The wilderness—the place of curse—becomes the place of rescue in more ways than one. For there, so the biblical story tells us, God made a home with his children to bless and shape them, to teach and enlighten them, to discipline and minister to them so that through them he could save the world. This opportunity to glory and rejoice over the wilderness in a final "going home" is open to us all—no exceptions.

PART I

The Wilderness

1

A FAITH
FOR GROWNUPS

---

*Therefore we will not fear, though the earth give way
and the mountains fall into the heart of the sea.*

PSALM 46:2

Several years ago I met two of the three sweet sisters for whom the world had collapsed and become a lightless planet. One of them, Lori, came home and found their mother, Mary Chandler, a deeply committed Christian, bound and strangled to death.

Five miles from where I live, a couple devoted to God and one another longed for a baby and prayed for one for some years. Imagine their excitement when they learned that the wife was nurturing a baby inside her. Imagine their devastation when the baby was born with severe spina bifida and other problems that meant it had a short, agonized life, leaving behind parents speechless with grief.

Another woman I know had spent more than thirty years in Asia as a missionary and was vacationing in America for a couple of weeks when she leaned over to pat a dog. The animal lunged at her, caught her by the mouth, and ripped away her whole bottom lip.

In the United Kingdom recently, two young boys took a two-year-old boy from a shopping mall, led him out to a secluded place, stoned him, then bludgeoned him to death before dragging his body onto a railway track, hoping to hide that he'd been savagely and cold-bloodedly murdered.

Atheism can never be proven philosophically, but the harsh, senseless, and horrific realities of daily living insinuate the absence of God more powerfully than any bankrupt philosophical argument can propose. In John 11, Martha unknowingly spoke the pain of millions when she said to the Lord, "If you had been here, my brother would not have died." Today countless hearts are saying to God, "If you'd been here, my mother, my child, my friend, my ———— would not have died or been mutilated."

Is it possible God isn't there at all?

Or if he is, does it make any difference? Is a world burdened down with personal tragedies, calamities, and wars—is a world like that worthy of God? Could a God worthy of respect, much less worship, allow such a world to exist if he could do anything about it?

Maybe that's it. Maybe Rabbi Harold Kushner and the many before him have it right; maybe God can't do anything about these horrors. Maybe he's as helpless as we are. Wishing us well, he wrings his handcuffed hands and feels bad that he can't help us. Poor God, what a fix to be in—to be impotent at a time like this.

What is it that generates so many questions in this area? I'm sure there are many factors, but this I know: As long as we continue to croon romantic ballads about God as a heavenly sweetheart (as the preacher Harry Emerson Fosdick would phrase it), we're going to have difficulties facing a planet that groans under a curse.

As long as ministers and authors continue to proclaim a God of fluff and gentility, we're not only ignoring the holy, loving God of Scripture, we're irreparably damaging the world he so loves that he wouldn't spare his own Son.

The deliberately one-sided picture we rightly paint of God for our little children in their very early years must be balanced as they grow. The content of a little child's faith isn't full enough to come to terms with Auschwitz, with the hellish reign of Papa Doc or Pol Pot. Adults must have their trusting heart, but their childish and limited view of God must be reworked and augmented. Scottish preacher W. M. Clow says we shouldn't want a childish faith, not only because we can't have it, but also because we can have something better!

By insinuating that a good God will only and always be gentle and tender, we're laying the foundation for a religion of sulk instead of gallantry, a grudging response from pouting lips instead of an enlightened and tough trust. No wonder Michael Medved, the film critic, insists that the one sound he hears rising daily from society is a whine. And, listen, it isn't coming only from the nonbelieving camp.

To assure a frightened four-year-old child that God won't let the bad man hurt him makes sense under the circumstances, but for ministers and authors to feed this unceasingly to people with their eyes open to the world we live in is shameless nonsense. And the shameless nonsense is only made more immoral by the ceaseless harping on favorite texts that "move us" by ministers who know better.

Such preaching and writing loses credibility. Only those whose lives are one long vacation can believe that stuff. What's more, it breeds a spirit of scorn in the prosperous and a spirit of resentment in the deprived. But more to the point, it's flat nonsense and biblically false!

So, what are we to do? Admit that God is a callous tyrant who is indifferent to the world's great wrongs and suffering? Pretend the horrors aren't real? Look at people enduring crucifixion and say, "Smile, God loves you"? So, what are we to do? Get God off the hook by blaming all the agony and tragedy on "bad luck" or demonic beings or free will gone mad?

Should we do what I recently heard a Bible professor say we should do? He suggested we should say nothing but get involved in people's pain, walk with them in their hurt. It's an interesting view to be put abroad by a Bible professor and, I suppose, as naive as any view you'll hear. There are no words that offer a framework for agony; the best we can do is make the best of it we can. This is what we should do? Kushner is right? There's no meaning in it, and since God doesn't make sense of it we are left to ourselves to invest it with meaning?

Not even the Bible professor can stick to his sermon—he talks. Besides, human sympathy and kindness aimed at alleviating the pain only underscores that God let the situation arise in the first place. Here we have it: Humans care and try to alleviate the suffering they can't eliminate, while God uncaringly stands by, watching. No wonder some people want to obey the second commandment, "love your neighbor," while dispensing with the first, "love the Lord your God." On this showing, speechless humans care more than the God who speaks in the Bible.

So, what are we to do? Should we deny the existence of "bad luck" (randomness, being in the wrong place at the wrong time) or the existence of malevolent forces that act in the human situation? Should we deny that God "allows" things to happen? I don't think we should deny any of that.

Should we say there are realities over which God has no control? Now that's something else!

In Northern Ireland some republican districts have signs painted on the walls: No RUC Here! The locals have forbidden the police (the Royal Ulster Constabulary) to enter; they've created no-go areas for the existing authorities. Is this what happens with God? Does human free will handcuff him? Is "chance" or randomness free of God's control? Do demonic beings roam the universe, wrecking and pillaging, as free agents who don't serve or answer to God? Are there no-go areas in the universe that exclude God?

Yes, but there's a day coming when God will assert his authority and gain control over everything, and the demons will pay. And in the meantime? The universe is not under God's control? Demons are not under God's control? "Natural law" is not under God's control? There are black holes where God is not? "No God here!"?

However complex all this is, maybe there's a way to see God in and through the curse the world staggers under; maybe there's a way to see him in and through it rather than just after it. Maybe we don't have to wring our hands in unrelieved bewilderment. It might be that God offers us the option to see suffering in all its forms as his redemptive work, and what we need is more courage to drink our share of the cup. We need the courage to see God as Job saw him.

2

BAD LUCK
OR DIVINE PLAN?

Who gave man his mouth? Who makes him deaf or mute?
Who gives him sight or makes him blind? Is it not I, the LORD?

EXODUS 4:11

Creation is under God's holy judgment! And what is God's "curse"? It's the expression of his holy anger. It isn't God's foaming at the mouth, using foul language, vindictive and vengeful, nor is it the expression of God's *loveless* holy anger—there's no such thing. God's holiness can never cause him to lose his heart!

God's curse is his holy love flowing toward humanity in redemptive anger. It's the holy Father withholding the tenderness of his holy love from his rebellious creation and chastising us because we are in mortal danger. His heart doesn't change toward us. That is, he loves us despite our crass selfishness and cruelty, and he pours out his anger to bring about our salvation. As Rabbi Abraham Heschel said: God's loving wrath is meant to destroy what made the wrath necessary in the first place.

To speak of God's curse on the earth as some spiteful, capricious, vicious reaction is to misunderstand God completely. But make no mistake, God's curse is the anger of an infinitely holy lover who makes known the price of rebellion.

Is God willing to put *a whole world* under curse? Yes he is, and if what Christians believe is true, he put Jesus Christ under the same curse, and he's worth more than the sum total of all the worlds you can imagine! If that's true, we'll hardly balk at saying that God put this world under a curse.

But would he curse the innocent and righteous along with the guilty? Would he do that? Christians won't bat an eye when they tell you he put someone innocent under the curse who was more than innocent; he put Jesus Christ under it, and he was positively full of holy righteousness and love.

Yes, but Jesus was only one person. Cursing an entire planet, generation after generation, is surely a more audacious move, isn't it?

The Christian faith doesn't see it that way. Christians dare to say that the death of this one person interprets all the suffering of the world, whether it's the suffering of the Holocaust, the gulags, or any other hellhole history tells us about. Christians say God's cursing of Jesus Christ, God the Son, gives us insight into the plight of the retarded boy or the girl with Down Syndrome, the murdered mother, or the disfigured missionary.

Did God place all creation (humanity included) under a curse? Yes, Genesis 3:14-19 tells us this, Paul in Romans 8:18-25 insists on it, and daily experience confirms the truth of it. Paul says:

> The creation waits in eager expectation for the sons of
> God to be revealed. For the creation was subjected to
> frustration, not by its own choice,...in hope that the

> creation itself will be liberated from its bondage to
> decay and brought into the glorious freedom of the
> children of God. (8:19-21)

The biblical message assures us that the same God who created out of joy-filled, holy love, blessing his creation, is the God who responded in holy love to judge humanity's sinful rebellion.[1] In creation he separated the waters into their places and made life to teem and flourish on earth. "Let there be an expanse between the waters to separate water from water. So God…separated the water under the expanse from the water above it" (Genesis 1:6-7). Then, in response to human sinfulness, God brought the waters back up over the earth in uncreation, and wholesale death occurred. "And the floodgates of the heavens were opened. And rain fell on the earth forty days and forty nights…. Every living thing that moved on the earth perished" (Genesis 7:11-12, 21).

God doesn't need us to get him off the hook by saying that he "permitted" the curse. He claims he brought it! The language of "permission" is legitimate enough; it's just not big enough to cover all the facts. And, besides, we need to remember that God *chooses* to allow what he allows.

Hidden behind the refusal of some of us to say God brought the curse is the suspicion that a good and caring God wouldn't do such a thing. If he did that, we think, he wouldn't be good or caring. But a good and caring God laid the sins of the world on his very own Son and brought about his crucifixion. God wasn't simply giving his permission then; he was positively carrying out his purpose.

Moreover, it's as hard to "defend" an all-powerful God who would "allow" Genghis Khan to bury eleven million Chinese, Great Britain to firebomb more than one hundred thousand civilians in Dresden and Hamburg, and the United States to do the same to one hundred thousand in Hiroshima. It's as hard to defend a God who would allow that kind of thing to go on generation after generation as it is to defend one who brings and sends nations against each other, as Isaiah says God does. Listen to this:

> Woe to the Assyrian, the rod of my anger,
>> in whose hand is the club of my wrath!
> I send him against a godless nation,
>> I dispatch him against a people who anger me,
> to seize loot and snatch plunder,
>> and to trample them down like mud in the streets.
> But this is not what he intends,
>> this is not what he has in mind;
> his purpose is to destroy,
>> to put an end to many nations. (10:5-7)

God sent Assyria to work his wrath on apostate Israel. That Assyria didn't think she was sent by God changes nothing. That Assyria didn't *mean* to do the will of God doesn't matter; she was doing it and God was sending Assyria to do it. Passages like this fill the pages of the prophets. When Habakkuk wants to know how God plans to judge the Judean gangsters and warlords, God tells him:

> Look at the nations and watch—
>> and be utterly amazed.

> For I am going to do something in your days
>> that you would not believe,
>> even if you were told.
> I am raising up the Babylonians,
>> that ruthless and impetuous people,
> who sweep across the whole earth
>> to seize dwelling places not their own. (1:5-6)

No wonder the prophet asks God to remember mercy while he is judging the nation.[2] In light of the horrors of war, no wonder he says, "I heard and my heart pounded, my lips quivered at the sound; decay crept into my bones, and my legs trembled" (3:16). But this holy judgment upon Israel by means of Babylonian invaders was the work of God. Babylon advanced in a cruel lust for power; what they didn't know was that they were carrying out the will of God.

It's perfectly legitimate, and even necessary at times, to carefully nuance what we mean when we say God has brought holy judgment on the world. What isn't legitimate, it appears to me, is to deny that he has done it. It's right to insist that those who commit brutal crimes are responsible for their hideous behavior, but we're not wise to exclude God from doing what he purposes *in* and *through* their wickedness. Regarding Jesus' crucifixion Peter said: "This man was handed over to you by God's set purpose and foreknowledge; and you, with the help of wicked men, put him to death by nailing him to the cross" (Acts 2:23).

If we hadn't rebelled against God, there'd be no suffering, no judgment against sin. But we *did* rebel, and God *did* bring holy and redemptive judgment on us, and until we face that truth we are missing a vital piece of the framework within which to live before God and one another.

When we talk of "bad luck," we mean that someone was in the wrong place at the wrong time. A person happened to be crossing the road just at the time the drunk driver was there or the stray bullet ricocheted and hit this child rather than that one. When we talk of bad luck, we mean that the specifics of the events weren't precisely planned; something about them could not be predicted. Should believers recognize such a thing as bad luck? Of course! The element of chance exists; no one of us could have predicted such events.

But the unpredictable exists because God created it. It suits his purposes that randomness exists; he wants it that way and insists that its reality be laid at his feet. He tells Job that he's the one who sends the rain on desolate land where no people dwell (Job 38:25-27). What a waste of water, we might think. But God chose to do it, whether we think it wise or not, and it was *God* doing it even though we would speak of it as unpredictable and random.

Sly King David gave orders to "allow" Uriah to be killed and then laid the brave man's death at the feet of bad luck.[3] If purpose and bad luck can go hand in hand with David, they can go hand in hand with God. First Kings tells us that God's purposed judgment on Ahab was carried out like this, "But someone drew his bow at random and hit the king of Israel between the sections of his armor" (22:34). Fancy that! A soldier, holding the horses, anxious to get a shot in, grabs his bow and shoots an arrow in the direction of the enemy "at random," and Ahab is judged. As he's driven away, someone might have been heard to mutter, "That was bad luck."

Something like a tornado blew down Job's house, and everybody knows that the path of tornadoes is unpredictable. Was it just bad luck? And the lightning that struck his crops and burned them up? More bad luck? And when God sends rain on the just and unjust, should we deny he does it because we can't ultimately say why the climatic conditions do this or that? All these things are under God's control, all are servants of God. All creation does God's bidding. Listen to this:

> Praise the LORD from the earth,
>> you great sea creatures and all ocean depths,
> lightning and hail, snow and clouds,
>> stormy winds that do his bidding,
> you mountains and all hills,
>> fruit trees and all cedars,
> wild animals and all cattle,
>> small creatures and flying birds,
> kings of the earth and all nations,
>> you princes and all rulers on earth.
>>> (Psalm 148:7-11)

We sing this in churches all over the land, and we need to take it seriously.

Random elements and aspects play a part in the matter of blessing as well as curse. We recognize this, but we insist on giving God the credit for the blessing; we don't just smile and call it good luck.

Speech like "good luck" or "bad luck" makes sense. We call a thing good or bad depending on whether we see it as a blessing or a curse. And we call it luck, meaning we couldn't have predicted it with precision; it could easily have happened to the guy standing next to us. As long as this is what we mean, such speech isn't harmful; but in practice it expresses a hidden conviction that some things are completely independent of God's control, and that simply isn't true.

When it rains hard and long on our fields that are in dire need of it, we thank God who sends the rain.[4] When that same rain destroys the business and home of our not-too-distant neighbor, we push God out the side door so he won't get bad press and then talk about bad luck and randomness.

We need to be careful what we're doing here. If you sit down and think about it, our lives—*all* our lives—hang together in an unending chain of "unpredictable" words, thoughts, and events. Before we know it, if we're not careful, we'll exclude our very lives from God's control. We can't predict a vast amount of life, but just because we're bound by ignorance and impotence, we're not to conclude that God is. God can accomplish his positive will by using what we call chance.

God has cursed creation and subjected it to futility. It now serves purposes it was never created for. As man rebelled against his Lord, not giving him his due, so the earth rebels against its lord, devouring its people. Under the curse of God the land refuses to bring forth food, famine smites the nations, and calamities decimate its peoples, Christians included.

I think it's important to frame our understanding of God's government of our world so that it will take into account the many different truths we read in Scripture and see in experience. It's important that we don't give any reality complete and utter autonomy, cutting it off from God's control and service.

In short, we need to frame our understanding of God's government of the world to allow for his overarching purpose to redeem his creation from sin, suffering, and futility.

3

SIMPLE ANSWERS
TO COMPLEX QUESTIONS

You are always righteous, O LORD, when I bring a case before you.
Yet I would speak with you about your justice: Why does the way
of the wicked prosper? Why do all the faithless live at ease?

JEREMIAH 12:1

It has been said that to every complex question there's a simple answer, and it's always wrong. Theologian Stanley Hauerwas doesn't lack confidence, but even he insists there are no simple answers. In fact, when it comes to pain, he confidently asserts there are no answers at all, but maybe that also is too simple. Memphis theologian John Mark Hicks is correct: There are no ultimately satisfying and exhaustive answers, but God hasn't left us completely in the dark. Still, we should be slow to give quick, easy answers to questions that have been asked for millennia.

Elsewhere and for other reasons, I've made mention of the movie *Glory*, which has as its central character Robert Gould Shaw, whose letters are stored in Washington, D.C. The son of a wealthy and prominent abolitionist, Shaw was commissioned as a colonel over the first African American regiment raised in the North during the Civil

War. The movie has many strong points to make, but for me the most compelling and uplifting element centers around the colonel and his lifelong friend, Thomas.

The movie presented Thomas as an articulate, confident, well-read young black gentleman who enjoyed "freedom" ("as did my father before me," he tells his fellow soldiers) and access to places of power. You can imagine how thrilled Thomas was to hear, after having grown up with him, that Robert was given the honor to command the regiment. Thomas was the first man to enlist and behind him came a host of others to sign up.

At first he felt free to engage Robert in happy conversation, to express his opinion on the food and how things were going, but the colonel soon made it clear there'd be no fraternizing between officers and the enlisted men. Robert forbade their mutual friend, a major, to act too friendly toward Thomas or any other soldier. This devastated Thomas. His pleasant, well-ordered world became a wilderness. The colonel's relationship with him was now shaped by his responsibility for the whole regiment. Thomas's heart was breaking, not because his friend was making a difference between him and the other enlisted men, but because he was *not* making a difference between them. Since the other men had never experienced the freedom Thomas grew up with or had been intimate with the regiment's leader, they weren't suffering the pain Thomas was enduring.

But it wasn't only Thomas who was hurting! The movie allows us to see what the hurting Thomas can't see very well—the colonel himself was heartbroken because his friend was hurting. *And this was true even though the colonel was inflicting the pain on Thomas.*

It's only later that the lovely Thomas sees the bigger picture and emotionally comes to terms with it. But he's a better man. The earlier Thomas was fine and noble and sensitive; the later Thomas was all that and more. He was stronger, more enlightened, and because he had the heart for it, he gladly though sadly embraced his situation along with his fellow soldiers. He entered into a fellowship with them he hadn't known before. So goes the movie and so goes life.

Good people, friends of God, in company with their innocent loved ones, can hardly help feeling anguish when God, who has shown himself to be their friend in Jesus Christ, doesn't give them preferential treatment. But while the anguish makes sense, if these good people can become convinced that their present loss is because God loves everyone, not just them, that he's working for the salvation and glory of an entire humanity—if they can be convinced of that, it will help them receive nobly the cup they have to drink.

It would be cruelly selfish of us to want God to love only us. If we didn't want him to love the whole world and pursue everyone as he has pursued us, we wouldn't be worthy of the name of Christ.

Not to want God to bless humanity is to want a lesser God than the one we have. Not only do we think less of ourselves when we self-ishly hoard, in our better moments we would think less of a God who could uncaringly dismiss the bulk of his created sons and daughters and make "pets" of us. No! We're pleased beyond measure that God will not close up his loving heart against any part of his creation.

But while we're wrestling with all that, if sometimes we feel as though we're Thomas, it might help us to note that the usual glib and abstract answers we hand out don't fit a concrete case of heartache. But the movie *Glory*, which is true fiction (if you know what I mean), helps us to see things we miss when we're working with mere arguments and abstractions. For example:

- The colonel wasn't punishing Thomas. He had done nothing wrong.
- Though Thomas learned a lot from the ordeal, the colonel hadn't subjected him to it just to teach him some special lesson. The colonel had in mind the regiment and not simply Thomas as an individual.
- The colonel hadn't ceased to be Thomas's friend; he'd become a friend to many others, and in a dangerous world, love experiences a conflict of interests.
- Thomas's pain was vicarious. Because he suffered that others might benefit, his pain was given a noble framework and a splendor that it couldn't have had if the suffering resulted from his own selfishness.
- The colonel was anything but callous; he was distressed by Thomas's great distress. A poignant scene in the movie makes that clear when the two lonely men, far from home, meet by accident on Christmas Eve night.
- Thomas found a new sense of brotherhood with his fellows as a result of the colonel's having their welfare in mind.

It wouldn't be difficult to tell the movie story differently. Ask the wrong questions, abstract bare facts from their setting, understate central factors, deny goodness of heart, isolate quotations, have no patience with the proposed larger picture, insist on individual rights while minimizing the importance and wonder of brotherhood—do all that and *Glory* isn't the powerful, compelling movie it is. Do all that to life, and life isn't the purpose-filled existence it can and should be.

Robert Gould Shaw's relationship with his friend Thomas enables us to look at God's relationship with humanity from a number of perspectives. Do take some time to reflect on this and give God the benefit of any doubts you may have. You would do that much for the colonel, even while you feel the pain of sweet-spirited, brave Thomas. And in all your reflection, think noble things of God.

4

GOD'S CURSE
AND LITTLE CHILDREN

"Do you hear what these children are saying?" they asked him.
"Yes," replied Jesus, "have you never read, 'From the lips
of children and infants you have ordained praise'?"

MATTHEW 21:16

When he was an older man, George Bernard Shaw raged against the Christian doctrine of atonement through the cross of Christ. He had Christ in mind when he insisted that he would have nothing to do with a religion that taught that God took pleasure in the death of a child. Jesus was hardly an old man when he died, so it isn't surprising that Shaw saw him as a child. At least Shaw felt the scandal of the doctrine, even if his understanding of it needed some fine-tuning.

Will God's curse fall on a child? He cursed his very own child. Paul does not hesitate to say that God "made him to be sin who knew no sin, so that in him we might become the righteousness of God" (2 Corinthians 5:21, RSV). He insists that Christ became a curse for us (Galatians 3:13).

Does God bring a child under his curse? Yes!

Is God punishing the baby because it's sinful? He is not. I don't share the view that a baby is sinful and is punished for it, and I'm certain that babies do no wrong, in light of Romans 9:11-12: "Though they were not yet born and had done nothing either good or bad, in order that God's purpose of election might continue, not because of works but because of his call, she was told" (RSV). So why would God bring an innocent baby under a curse that he introduced because of sin?

In Amos 4:5-6 God tells Israel that he brought famine on them because they had turned from him, so we know the suffering generated by the famine was punishment for guilt. But any babies born during the famine suffered along with the guilty. The suffering introduced by God is indeed penal suffering, and a newborn baby shares that judgment with the guilty. God is not only prepared to subject the baby to judgment, the Scriptures tell us he has done it again and again.

But we need to be clear about it: God does not level his wrath against a baby itself. A baby is no sinner and isn't punished for its sin;[1] but that same innocent child does share the hurt that guilty sinners have brought down on themselves. So, if we ask if a suffering child is being punished, the answer must be no; but if we ask if the child is bearing the hurt that is indeed penal suffering, the answer's yes.

If they could have spoken, the children in Amos's day would have said to the apostate in Israel: "This is my body which is given for you." Guilty Israel might have maligned God when they saw their babies suffering, but before they looked to lay blame on God, they needed to admit that their treachery triggered his holy chastisement. A world full of wickedness called down penal suffering, and Israel's children bore it with them.

Disabled and robbed children, who share with us the hurt of the curse we helped prompt, have much to tell us if only we can hear. For all our technology and sense of our own godhood, we can't stave off their hurt and their deprivation. They look at us without knowing it and say: "And you? You are gods? Never! You aren't gods and we're the living proof that you aren't. We and millions like us in every generation." They expose our original sin of pride and stupidity when we professed ourselves to be wise and became fools.

And when we humans want to distance ourselves from their hurt, when we want to blame bad luck or stupid doctors or nameless viruses, demonic thugs, or perverted free will, these hurting children silently convict us, saying: "We're like this because you by your evil have brought down the curse of God upon us all."

Rereading that last sentence prompts me to say again: God's judgment against our sin is not vindictiveness or spite! It isn't that we sin and God burns the children. He's a relentless lover pursuing us with the intention of giving us the fullness of a glorious life. To do that, he has brought a curse down on us all, not only because of our sin, but also because of his ceaseless and loving longing for us. Our guilt has brought God's curse not only on the guilty but also on the innocent: Jesus Christ and a host of innocents.

The curse is one of God's ways to deal with sin. As long as we make suffering the supreme calamity, we're ignoring something God thinks is more basic—the sin factor. As long as we make suffering the supreme concern, the astounding sacrifice of the countless innocents is lost on us. God puts them to grief so that we might repent with deep contrition, so that we might shoulder the responsibility for the fragmentation and hurt of the world. They plead with us to open our hearts as well as our eyes. Together with the righteous who lie slain in our homes and streets, together with the vulnerable who are used by vice lords and drug barons, these precious people call us to see suffering as more than a social problem. They call us to see more than medical challenges. They call us to see suffering as a fruit of humanity's willful rebellion against God. They call us to see how we've "driven" an infinitely holy lover to pursue us with pain, not because he foams at the mouth in vengefulness, but because he can't bear to see us go to eternal destruction.[2] To keep us from eternal loss, he subjects us to the terrible rigors of the curse.

Before we protest that the curse is overkill, before we complain that the whole of humanity should not be put to grief just to deal with the sin factor, we need to remember what God is after—the redemption and glorification of an entire humanity. And he isn't simply interested in fine-tuning our lives, he's interested in saving us—saving us eternally and clothing us with an internal and external glory that's presently beyond our comprehension.

In the end we've got to say that if God thinks the glory-filled end justifies the grief-laden means, then the choice is clear: We can trust God and justify him as we make our pilgrimage through this wilderness life, or we can tell him we aren't prepared to accept his redemptive scheme and rage against him at every turn.

In the meantime, children in the tens of thousands are suffering terribly. We can distance ourselves from their plight, saying we have no responsibility (when in truth, we are responsible), or we can look at them with nothing but pity (which masks the more profoundly important response they're wanting to generate—repentance toward God). We can talk of bad luck or demonic thugs, lack of medical research or human social awareness. This might serve to shift the blame from us as sinners, but it misses the central point of their vicarious suffering. To look at the suffering children with nothing but pity in our hearts is to miss the message they bring to us from God: "This is my body which is given for you!" If we look at their tragedy-filled lives and feel nothing but sadness, we create another tragedy, one that beggars description. If the children knew we were filled with pity for them, they might say, "Yes, yes, we know you're sorry for us, but that isn't enough! Hear and see the other things we're saying and showing to you."

I can't remember where I came across the following story, nor can I remember the details, but it struck me as conveying a brave and lovely truth along with its fiction.

It seems there were thousands of "baby souls" waiting in heaven to be born into human life on earth, and God called them all together. "I need volunteers," he said, and every little soul clamored to be given the chance to do God a service because they knew, since it was God's will, it must be good.

"I need some of you to be born into prosperous families, to live long, full lives in healthy bodies and minds. I need you to remind humans how I bless them, and I need you to use your influence and rich lives to my glory and for the benefit of many who are deprived. I will be with you throughout your long and successful lives."

Every little being was wide-eyed with excitement and begged for the privilege to go.

Then God said, "I also need many of you to be born into deprived families, and to suffer much at the hands of wicked parents, crooked governments, and greedy foreign investors. I need many of you to live in bodies that are only half finished or that are defective. For some of you, your time on earth will be brief and others of you will wish they were brief. I want you to use your great power and influence to show humans their awful sin and to tell them that, because I love them, I can't just let them go on in their sin. That's why you will be suffering. And I will be with you every moment of your pain-filled lives."

Without exception, every little soul was wide-eyed with excitement and begged for the privilege to go.

So, the next time you look at some darling child...

5

IS GOD A HEAVENLY
HIT MAN?

---

*The LORD is compassionate and gracious, slow to anger,
abounding in love. He will not always accuse, nor will he harbor
his anger forever; he does not treat us as our sins deserve....
He knows how we are formed, he remembers that we are dust.*

PSALM 103:8-10,14

There's nothing sadistic about God. He doesn't rise in the morning, stretch, and decide to target some poor victim, or tens of thousands of victims, before getting around to "saving the world." God is not a heavenly hit man who enjoys his work, but he's deadly earnest about the glorious galactic redemption he is accomplishing. And he is willing to pay the price, *whatever* it costs—to himself and to us—to get that task completed.

As soon as we divorce world suffering from the one who brought it about in response to our sin, *of course* it makes suffering more difficult, if not impossible, to work with. Seeing God as *Father* of us all, as he is revealed in his *Son* Jesus Christ, gives us a framework to work within. It's a father we have to contend with and not merely a judge; a father does the judging. It isn't an impersonal force that subdues us or a stranger who has no commitment to us or a foster parent who has no affection for us. It's our holy, loving Father, for pity's sake!

Whenever we speak of God's cursing all of creation, it's easy to leave the impression that he gets some perverse pleasure out of human suffering. This just isn't true. "In all their distress he too was distressed" (Isaiah 63:9). When Israel was outrageously wicked during the period of the judges, and God was compelled to punish them, he finally went to their rescue because "he could bear Israel's misery no longer" (Judges 10:16). Then there's that lovely passage that says Jesus "took up our infirmities and carried our diseases" (Matthew 8:17). In the person of Jesus Christ, the compassionate God first took these burdens upon his heart and then proceeded to cure them.

It seems to me that it's mainly scholars and thinkers who raise all the difficult questions and offer all the complex answers about the state of God's mind when he subjects us to the curse. It is true that the sufferers of the world often rage against God, scream in their agony, sulk in their pain, or brood in their silence—all that, but then they make it up with God again. And why do they? Why do the sufferers make it up with God again, despite having no satisfying answers? Because down in their bones they can't believe that God is a sadistic brute. More to the point, a host of them in every generation have come to believe that the Father of us all is like Jesus Christ, and if he's like Jesus Christ, there must be something wondrous being accomplished by means of the curse. And Jesus himself, while he was bearing the curse on the cross, assured them that they're right; something wondrous *is* being accomplished through the curse.

Maybe if we knew what is at stake, maybe if we understood the nature of sin *in light of the holy love of God,* maybe then we could understand why God touched humanity and the whole of creation with such severe judgment. Maybe we'd understand better why, instead of Eden, we live in the wilderness; why, instead of living in untouched paradise, we live in a jungle. If we knew that God is keeping unbroken pleasure from us and subjecting us to the curse *so that* he might redeem us from a humanity-damning plague, perhaps we'd gut it out better and give him glory.

I can understand nonbelievers finding it difficult to comprehend how the curse is part of our redemption; what's harder to fathom is why followers of the once-crucified Lord Jesus Christ refuse to believe it. The curse on humanity comes into focus in the Christ of the cross. There it burns more fiercely than at any time or in any place in the universe. It is in the cursed Christ of the cross that world redemption and glorification are gained.

Christ bore the curse, which is God's judgment against humanity's sin. Without that judgment and Christ's holy acceptance of it on humanity's behalf, there is no salvation or glorification. When we see Christ's holy submission to that condemnation of sin, our eyes are opened, our hearts are pierced, and repentance is generated. His bearing our sin by becoming a curse for us proclaims the love of the holy Father who sent him, and love like that draws us. It isn't just God's holiness and righteousness that the once-cursed Christ exhibits, it's the holy and righteous *love of a Father* that's a placard for the world to see. Through the judgment, mercy is being offered; in the righteousness of judgment, holy love is seen. God's sternness is also his tenderness.

Scripture proclaims this message over and over. Hosea spoke to an apostate northern kingdom, Israel, and told them that despite their great wickedness, God couldn't give them up. He pictures God as a father who walks the floor, wondering what to do with a son who will simply not turn from his treacherous ways or a husband whose wife just won't remain faithful. The father/husband concludes that punishment must follow. Israel is to be subjected to foreign invasion and exile.

But what is the point of Israel's pain and chastisement? Why the punishment? About the nation that has gone after other lovers and forgotten God, the Lord says, "Therefore I am now going to allure her; I will lead her into the desert and speak tenderly to her. There I will give her back her vineyards, and will make the Valley of Achor a door of hope. There she will sing as in the days of her youth" (Hosea 2:14-15).

Note the boldness of this declaration, and while you're doing that, note that the words are spoken as if nothing strange was being said. God says he's going to allure her, not by bringing her to the Garden of Eden, but by bringing her into the wilderness. It's in the wilderness, he tells us, that he'll "speak tenderly" to her. *Are we able to hear this?* The word of God in the wilderness is God speaking tenderly! Reflect for a moment on the clash of these two images. God brought the children of Israel into a place of desolation so that he could allure them by speaking tenderly to them.

God goes on to say he will make "the Valley of Achor" a door of hope. You might remember the history connected with Achor (Joshua 6:15–7:26). Israel had just entered Canaan to take it over; the land was filled with hostile nations. God assured them that he would make them victorious, and yet at the little town of Ai the army of Israel was repulsed. Panic swept through the nation and then they discovered that a leader, Achan, had violated the ban. They took Achan into the Valley of Achor and stoned him. They named the place "Achor," the valley of "troubling," because of the judgment that

Achan's sin had generated. In this reference to the Valley of Achor, God is telling Israel that he will bring her through hard times in order to woo her and that she would end up singing rather than mourning (Hosea 2:15). As it was with Israel, so it is with us all.

Our wilderness experience doesn't simply tell us how badly we've offended God, it's also a measure of his earnestness when he says, "I will redeem you, I will save you!" How earnest is God in his purpose to redeem us from sin? Earnest enough to subject us to pain that purges us. Earnest enough to put us to grief to open our eyes. Earnest enough to burn into our souls that we aren't self-sufficient, that we're totally dependent on him for everything. The wilderness, if we have the heart to bear it and the trust to live in hope there, is another of God's ways of taking us seriously. So anxious is he to live with and love us that he subjects us to the curse of the wilderness, subjects himself to it as well, and finally, in Jesus Christ, he experiences the curse to the full, draining the cup, and experiencing in the Son the full meaning of abandonment. That God bothers to do any of that should make us stagger, not only at what it says about him but us. Who are we and who does God intend us to be that he engages with us in these ways?

Listen, it's because God thinks so much of us that he subjects us to so much trouble. Isn't that what C. S. Lewis had in mind when he said a great artist won't trouble himself much if he's sketching to amuse or please a child, but if he were doing a portrait that is to reflect his life's work, well, that'd be a different story? He'd subject the painting to hard labor and wouldn't settle for less. So it is with God, who is working on his "masterpiece"—glorified humanity.

No, God's not a heavenly hit man who enjoys his work. He's the holy Father who adores his children and is bringing them to glory.

6

OUR FELLOW PILGRIM

The LORD said, "I will go with you, and I will give you victory."
Moses replied, "If you do not go with us, don't make us leave
this place. How will anyone know that you are pleased
with your people and with me if you do not go with us?"

EXODUS 33:14-16 (TEV)

Between the utterly impassive God who feels absolutely nothing and the God who appears to be an emotional roller coaster, weeping oceans of tears but mostly partying a lot with a few friends while the bulk of the world dies in silent agony—between those two gods is the God of the Scriptures.

If you can believe in a God who misses you when you're gone, longs for you when you're away, gets angry for appropriate reasons, and does what's necessary for you to get his message, you can believe God is our fellow pilgrim in the wilderness.

But it does take some believing. It isn't like saying some high-ranking statesman shared a cup of coffee with us or a Supreme Court justice spent the day among us at our summer encampment. That would be worth bragging about, of course, but claiming that God is with us every single day, as close as our heartbeat, as we make our way through this often tear-filled life—now that claim is of a different order. There has to be something solid to ground that on. Well, there is! There's the incarnation of God who came to us not only *in* Jesus Christ but *as* Jesus Christ. In doing this he made visible to us the truth that he had been whispering and hinting at down the millennia. "Leave you alone? Abandon you? Not me; I long to be with you."

But just because that truth is firmly established, it's no less astonishing. It's the kind of truth you disbelieve for the joy it brings.[1] It's the sort of thing that might lead you to say to yourself, "It can't be, but…it is." And that's just how G. K. Chesterton put it in his poem *The House of Christmas,* which tells of the blessed God's coming to be with us in the child, Jesus of Nazareth. Here's the final verse:

> *To an open house in the evening*
> *Home shall men come,*
> *To an older place than Eden*
> *And a taller town than Rome.*
> *To the end of the way of the wandering star,*
> *To the things that cannot be and that are,*
> *To the place where God was homeless*
> *And all men are at home.*[2]

To the place where God was homeless. Isn't that a lovely way to put a profoundly lovely truth? That breathtaking truth was foreshadowed for us when God chose to dwell in the midst of Israel.

"Have them make a sanctuary for me, and I will dwell among them," says God in Exodus 25:8. The tabernacle was a massive tent, made of skins and wooden boards. Because Israel was always on the move and God had chosen to move with them, the tabernacle needed to be a temporary structure, one that could be set up and taken down as the Israelites moved from place to place. It was the home of a pilgrim, a sort of divine mobile home.

The most sacred piece of furniture in the tabernacle, the ark of the covenant, spoke powerfully of God's *presence with* Israel. It stood alone in the Holy of Holies and contained the tables of the covenant, the mercy seat (the lid of the ark/box) where atonement for the nation was made and where the glory of God, the Shekinah, manifested itself. The ark had four rings, two on each side, and through these, two poles were positioned so the ark could be carried. To ensure that the ark was always ready for travel, no one ever removed the poles, even when the ark sat in the sanctity of the Holy of Holies. Everything about the tabernacle, the ark of the covenant included, spoke of movement rather than a settled condition.

Yahweh was a pilgrim among pilgrims, sharing their hardships.[3]

Because God's personality is very complex, we can affirm things about him that on the surface look like contradictions. For instance, Lamentations 3:32-33 reads: "Though he brings grief, he will show compassion, so great is his unfailing love. For he does not willingly bring affliction or grief to the children of men." Even if God willingly distresses people, he doesn't do it willingly.

A fine surgeon would rather not perform surgery; he would rather we didn't need it. But if we do, he does it willingly. So God is willing to bring grief, but he'd rather not. In our distress, he, too, is distressed.[4]

I'm saying all of this to make the point that talk about God's sharing our suffering isn't just pious sentiment. If we can believe in a holy Father who loves us, we can believe in a holy Father who feels our pain as part of his own. We see the truth of this illustrated before our very eyes in time of war.

Was it only the troops who went off to Europe to fight in the wars? Was it only the military who ran halfway round the world to brawl in Korea or Vietnam? Where were those who loved the soldiers with all their hearts, who would gladly have swapped places with them to keep them from danger—where do we think they were? Where there are lovers, there is no *absolute* parting. Hearts at home endured the heat and the cold, the pain and the fear of their faraway loved ones. Do we suppose it was only the prodigal who went to the far country? Hardly! His hurting father's heart went with him. Sweethearts and parents, family and friends don't stay at home. The most important part of them, their heart, leaves home when the beloved ones go away. What's true of human lovers at their best is true of God.

Read the book of Hosea and tell me God doesn't hurt at our pain—even when we've brought it on ourselves! In his home Hosea learned the gospel of the love of a holy Lord. The whole northern kingdom, Israel, was departing from God and going after Baal, and God says, "The land is guilty of the vilest adultery in departing from the LORD" (1:2). He commands the prophet to marry Gomer, a girl shaped by society. The prophet knows the first baby is his, and he calls it Jezreel ("God sows or scatters," meaning that God has given the baby but also that he will scatter the kingdom). The second baby is a daughter, but Hosea isn't sure she's his, and consequently he doesn't feel the same about the child. He calls the little girl Lo-ruhamah (she who "is not loved" or who "has not received mercy"). Of the third baby, he's certain: the little boy isn't his, and so he calls him LoAmmi ("no kin of mine"). The children map out the apostasy of Israel: Israel was God's in the beginning, began to drift, and finally departed from God.

Gomer leaves home and ends up in some form of slavery.[5] It's easy to imagine some friend of the prophet, one who knows about Gomer's unfaithfulness, coming to tell him the story of her trouble. "Hosea," he might say, "I know Gomer has broken your heart, but I just want to tell you she has finally got what she deserves. I was in Debir only the other day on business and there she was, being sold into service." The prophet might have thanked him, hurried his friend off, and quickly made his way to Debir because that's where his heart was! Hosea sought her out and bought her out of her self-made trouble because he loved her. In doing this for love of his wayward wife, Hosea learned the gospel of the love of God for his wayward people.

I'm wanting to make the point that God can't stand by unfeeling when his children peevishly, spitefully, and selfishly slam the door of their home behind them on their way into the dark. His children are all tangled up in his heartstrings.

While standing at the door to Canaan, Moses made the same point to the Israelites: "There [in the desert] you saw how the LORD your God carried you, as a father carries his son, all the way you went until you reached this place" (Deuteronomy 1:31). God may not take our burdens on his body (though see 1 Peter 2:21), but he certainly takes them on his heart. He tells Israel, "When you pass through the waters, I will be with you" (Isaiah 43:2). When Joseph was in prison, "the LORD was with him" (Genesis 39:21), and when Saul persecuted the Jews, Christ came and wanted to know, "Saul, Saul, why do you persecute me?" (Acts 9:4). In Matthew 25:34-45 Christ tersely says, in essence, "When you turned them down, you turned me down!" And in warm approval he says, "When you did it to them, you did it to me!"

God has never been a mere spectator! And when he comes to us in Jesus of Nazareth, he enters fully into our lives, which is why we find him astonished at the unbelief of people (Mark 6:6) and—it's a marvelous truth to tell—astonished at the existence and richness of the faith of a nonelect Gentile (Luke 7:9).

This tent-dwelling Lord *intends* to be understood as a pilgrim with his people. When David presumes to build God a permanent structure, God for his own reasons agrees to have one, but he reminds David that the need isn't *his*. Here's what he says: "I have not dwelt in a house from the day I brought the Israelites up out of Egypt to this day. I have been moving from place to place with a tent as my dwelling. Wherever I have moved with all the Israelites, did I ever say to any of their rulers…, 'Why have you not built me a house of cedar?'" (2 Samuel 7:6-7). It's part of the glory of God that he chooses to travel with his people and share their unsettled state.

What if it turns out that this almighty God, powerful enough simply to *will* constellations into existence, majestic beyond human imagination—what if this God actually *delights* in humans? *Longs* to share our joys and troubles? Is *eager* to take our pain on his heart? What if, *to make sure we come through to life eternal,* he actually became human and tabernacled among us? Listen, not only tabernacled in a body, but tabernacled among us. And by "us" I mean humanity. He came to the world!

"Yes, yes, all very interesting and charming, Jim. Now, could you pass the salt, please?" But what if God really *does* delight in us? What if we could see him now, and he really is looking at us as a father or mother looks at the child they love and are proud of? What if he really does have a mother's heart and grieves when we get ourselves in trouble? What if it's true that he sees us, not only sinful, but victimized by superior powers—vicious, brutalizing, merciless powers—and has come to rescue us? It's what holy mothers do and feel and see.

Henry Ward Beecher once said that he found God when he realized that his mother would move heaven and earth to rescue him from trouble even if that trouble was of his own making. God can do no less than a holy mother. The truth is, we may want to shut God out of our lives, but he can't shut himself out of them, can't be content to be left out and just leave it at that. Robed in flesh, God the Son weeps over a city that is ruining itself by rejecting him (Luke 19:41-45). If any of us has tried in vain to bring home a sinning child or husband or wife, one we loved more than life itself, we know why God's chest was heaving and great sobs were bursting from him. *He can't stay away from us.*

So, what if his gentle and implicit rebuke of David in 2 Samuel 7:5-7 should be taken with utmost seriousness since it was startlingly confirmed in the Incarnation. What if he was saying: "Do you think I'm impressed with people flocking around me? What thrills me is to be down among the people. One day, you'll see, I'll be going into their houses, eating meals with them, weeping and laughing with them. It's the give and take of joyful, honorable life with people that truly delights me. To be enshrined in their worship and enthroned on their praise is right, and it's essential for them, but fullness of life with them is what I'm after."

And if God, the chief pilgrim, is present with us as a fellow pilgrim, we'll want our lives to confess that. We'll want our lives to honor the kind of pilgrimage we're on—a pilgrimage of life moving toward fullness of life.

Be that as it may, while God's presence as our fellow pilgrim makes demands of us, those demands come from someone who has cast his lot with us against all the forces of wickedness and destruction in the heavens and on earth. Whatever is asked of us, it's asked by one who honors us by his company, inspires us with his presence and assures us with these words, "Never will I leave you; never will I forsake you" (Hebrews 13:5).

Say that isn't true, say it's too good to be true, say it's utter nonsense; but don't say it's dull, don't say it's all one big yawn. In this big, round, teeming, chaotic, noisy, pain-filled world, there can't be more exciting news than this: *God is with us in it all!*

PART II

❮❮❮

The People
of the Wilderness

7

LIZZIE EATON'S SCALES

I am the LORD, who exercises kindness, justice
and righteousness on earth, for in these I delight.

JEREMIAH 9:24

Books like this have more than their share of heroic stories about lives lived in dramatic splendor. But before I get carried away in praise of bravery perhaps something needs to be said in praise of "the ordinary," because that's what the greater part of our lives is made up of—the ordinary rather than the heroic.

The sensitive and brilliant A. B. Davidson, a Scottish theologian of a few generations ago, said that a person's most difficult challenge is to continue to do well the ordinary, daily things of life. And yet this is exactly what God asks of us. He wants his pilgrim people to be solid, dependable, and consistently good in all our relationships as we make our way through this chaotic and restless world. He wants us to give a rich, warm, fair, and even generous response to the people around us, and he wants us to do it in his name. We please God by making the desire to please and enjoy him the dynamic that shapes all the areas of our lives.

Proverbs tells us: "The LORD abhors dishonest scales, but accurate weights are his delight" (11:1).[1] You might be surprised at how often this kind of speech is in God's mouth in the Old Testament. God implicitly threatens exile if people won't be fair in their dealings with others.[2] He not only said it was wrong for Israel to use dishonest scales, he also said it was wrong for them to have dishonest scales in their houses since lying scales can only be used for one thing—cheating. If you buy or make dishonest scales it means you intend to cheat and to continue to do so, which is even worse.

But this speaks only to the first part of Proverbs 11:1. The second half of the verse really rings my bell without weakening the first: God delights in accurate weights! Say it to yourself a few times; say it out loud. "God delights in accurate scales."

When I was a boy, digital scales were unknown. Most stores had scales with a bright, shiny, scooped container (usually polished brass) on one end and iron or brass weights on the other. The sweets, lentils, grains, or whatever went into the dish and various weights were put on the other side to balance the scale. I loved to see Lizzie Eaton, who ran a local mom-and-pop store, doing her magic with the tiny weights and shiny scoop.

Lizzie had a reputation for having honest scales; her scales were *always* honest. Her aim to be good wasn't a passing desire; hers was a habitual and consistent goodness. It didn't make any difference what workday it was, Monday through Saturday she had honest scales. Whether those who came were poor or rich, ignorant or wise, pretty or plain, popular or disliked, they were all given a glad-hearted fairness.

Lizzie's honest scales were a daily protest against all ugly favoritism, a protest against all snobbery and artificial divisions, and a rejection of all peevishness and spite. No matter who you were, you could get a square deal from Lizzie.

All that pleased me, but *God enjoyed Lizzie's scales even more than I did.*

I can imagine God wandering into the mom-and-pop stores all over the world, leaning on the counter and beaming as he checks the scales. Admiring the shine, testing the many weights, from the smallest to the largest. "Perfect, just perfect!" I can hear him saying with a warm glance at the proprietor. It's easy, then, for me to imagine him patting Lizzie's shoulder and telling her, "This is good work you're doing, Lizzie."

This is more than sober approval, more than a solemn judgment. Proverbs 11:1 speaks of delight! God isn't bent over and smiling at a legalist-run scale. He can't delight himself in what isn't generous, but given generosity and compassion, he is easily pleased. We can see this in the way he instructed the Israelites in Leviticus 19. He insists that they leave the edges of their fields unharvested so the poor can help themselves, but he didn't define what the "edge" was. He might have, but he didn't. Instead, he gave them the commandment and then—repeatedly—reminded them who he was, "I am the LORD your God" who brought you out of Egypt. He was calling them to generosity; the message was, "Treat others as I have treated you." We are not merely to treat people as we would wish they'd treat us, we are called to treat others as God has already treated us and continues to treat us.

God delights in accurate weights. Like a little boy who finds a harmless insect and brings it in to his mom with wide-eyed delight (the little boy, I mean) to show it off, to hear her oohs and aahs, wanting her to share in his pleasure. He says, "See? Isn't it lovely? Look how…" and on he goes. Like a young man who brings home his young woman so his dad can wonder at her and be greatly pleased with her—so God delights in accurate weights. As a young bride is beside herself with delight that the wedding was perfect, that everyone turned up on time, that everything went smoothly and everyone was breathless at how lovely it was—so God delights in warm, honest, above-board people and their way of relating to others.

This isn't always the message we hear. Some give the impression that life has to be a prolonged martyrdom to get God's attention. Others seem to say that ceaseless meditation and prayer is the only way to truly get close to God. It's true that when it's needed he can raise up someone to do extraordinary things—things that take our breath away with the drama and sacrificial nature of them. At times he'll point us to some prayer warrior who'll drive us to our knees. In the meantime, we need to take note that the everyday things of life, well done, set him smiling and make his day.

Notice how Paul can proclaim the resurrection, the death of Death and the grave of the Grave, in one breath and in the next sentence say, "Now, about the collection for God's people..." (1 Corinthians 15:54–16:10). Paul speaks of the very foundations of the Christian faith, and then, without a hint that he's changing gear to some lower level, he speaks of the benevolence planned for poor Christians in Jerusalem. He takes us from eternal truth of galactic proportions to the down-to-earth matter of how benevolence should be carried out. He isn't embarrassed to link the everyday issues with the eternal once-for-all matters.

We can see this linkage everywhere we look, in the Bible and out of it. Take the case of Holocaust survivor Viktor Frankl, who was subjected to the torture of medical experimentation: surgery without anesthetics, surgery under the guise of furthering knowledge. He hated every bit of it, of course, but there were other aspects of life in a concentration camp that almost drove him over the edge of reason into lunacy.

The guards in the camp would round up the prisoners early in the mornings and march them out in the bitter cold to some barren stretch to dig trenches. It was just another piece of torment because the trenches they dug one day they'd have to fill in the next. As the guards marched them out into the freezing wilderness, they'd yell at them to move faster. They'd beat the inmates if they were too slow and left many of them on the road, nursing their wounds and freezing to death. When they got to the site and began digging, the guards would scream at them and curse them. There were more beatings, more insults, and the never-ending screaming into their faces, "Hurry up! Faster, faster, you lazy pigs!"

Something about that almost unhinged Frankl. *Hurry for what?* The absolute single-mindedness of that cruelty seized him. The sheer, deliberate, manufactured pointlessness of it all. It was all agony—the starvation, the pitiless marches in boots too small or in bare or rag-wrapped feet, the digging with frozen hands and poor equipment, the beatings from the enemy, and the stealing and killing that went on among the pain-crazed captives. But the guard's face, stuck right into theirs, screaming at the top of his lungs, "Hurry up, you lazy Jewish pig!"—that was the brink of the abyss.

But in the middle of all this forced betrayal and chosen corruption, Frankl discovered "a pair of honest scales." They came in the form of another inmate who was usually one of the servers at meal-times. As soon as they were herded into the hut, Frankl looked to see if this man was there. This particular prisoner served the meal with his head down, raised only enough to see the plate but never the face of the person he was serving. Why? He didn't want to see the person he was serving in case it was someone he didn't like, and he would be tempted to give that person less. He didn't want to see someone he liked in case he gave him more than his share and someone else was deprived. No matter who stood before him, it was in this man's heart to treat that person fairly.[3]

There in the middle of hell was a word from heaven. There in the absence of humanity was a human heart. For Frankl it was more than the food, maybe least of all the food; it was the humanity, the fairness, the rightness, the strength and glory of this man's heart. His behavior defied the power of moral chaos. His was a purposed goodness, a living fairness, working its marvelous work, keeping people alive in a wilderness without pity and where justice was a stranger.

I think about that unnamed prisoner and feel a warm jealousy rising in me. Knowing me, I know that I couldn't rise and couldn't have risen to that height under those circumstances, but I want to be like this man in my own easier circumstances.

In a world where there's more than enough treachery and meanness to go around, it's great to know that God is pleased to the point of delight with dependably honorable people who work from honest scales. And if God can see our mom-and-pop lives, see our accurate scales that speak of consistent goodness and a glad-hearted fairness for everyone, and be tickled pink by it, what does that tell us? It says that when we live out the glory of the ordinary, we're like God himself. In Judah the rich and powerful, the wise and wonderful were boasting in their assets, but God sends out this word, "Let him who boasts boast about this: that he understands and knows me, that I am the LORD, who exercises kindness, justice and righteousness on earth, for in these I delight" (Jeremiah 9:24).

The message throughout Scripture is this: Treat others as God has treated us and continues to treat us. "Do not oppress an alien; you yourselves know how it feels to be aliens, because you were aliens in Egypt" (Exodus 23:9). God sends sunshine and rain on both the righteous and the wicked, and he commands us to love our enemies (Matthew 5:43-48). Even our enemies are to know that we work with honest scales and accurate weights—that we will treat them with glad-hearted fairness. And maybe if we can be fair, we can be kind, and from there we can become friendly and affectionate.

One of the beauties of consistent goodness in everyday living is that it gives assurance and challenge in the midst of bedlam and change. The foundations for a God-glorifying life seem to be swept away in the chaos of cynicism and cheating, but one set of honest scales operated day by day by one honorable man or woman defies the erosion and helps the strugglers to believe that goodness is possible and is to be expected even in "the wilderness."

8

THE TRIUMPH OF TRUST

Though He slay me, yet will I trust Him.

JOB 13:15 (NKJV)

Israel had been encamped in the wilderness for a year at the foot of Mount Sinai when Moses gave this grand invitation to his brother-in-law, Hobab:

> "We are setting out for the place about which the
> LORD said, 'I will give it to you.' Come with us and we
> will treat you well, for the LORD has promised good
> things to Israel."
>
> He answered, "No, I will not go; I am going back
> to my own land and my own people."
>
> But Moses said, "Please do not leave us. You know
> where we should camp in the desert, and you can be
> our eyes. If you come with us, we will share with you
> whatever good things the LORD gives us." (Numbers
> 10:29-32)

This is a glorious offer, and when we remember where Moses is when he makes it, we see even better its boldness and grandeur. If rocks could cry out, they'd have said, "Everything is against you, Moses! The wilderness, the pitiless heat, the unending glare, the bitter cold nights, the size of your company and their lack of character. These people will break your heart; they'll provoke God beyond endurance. How will they eat and drink? How will they overcome their enemies? You have no war-trained armies, no influential friends or political clout. Everything's against you. Your personal limitations, the vast complex of logistical difficulties involved. As far as the eye can see, all the way to the rim of the world—everything's your enemy. Do you hear? The whole world's against you! How can you expect 'good things'?"

Isn't this what so much of life cries out to us, Christian and non-Christian alike? "Everyone and everything is against you! The powers that be, the insinuating cancer, the arguments, the wrecked marriage, the baby shoes that were never worn, the spindly legged children with their distended bellies and sunken eyes, the recurring seizures, the stubborn local authorities who defend the wicked status quo, the unanswered questions, the bedlam of the cities, the empty church buildings and dwindling congregations—all against you! Your speech is pathetic, your skills are meager, and your opposition is well entrenched."

In our saner moments, we know all that's true. Everyone and everything *is* against us. When was it any different? When *wasn't* the world against us? The people of God who hold out hope for a harassed humanity have never triumphed over evil powers or adversity because they had political clout or a monopoly on wisdom or brilliance. They have triumphed because they had something better. They had God.

You've seen God's power in your own life, haven't you? Don't you remember when you were in such pain that you were sure you'd never survive? And yet here you are, still with God, still listening for his voice, and still praising his name. Haven't you been so frustrated by sin's victories over you that you thought you'd never be free? And now you can't remember exactly when you overcame that besetting sin, but you rejoice knowing it's a thing of the past.

And listen, God is good even to those who haven't yet taken on the name of Christ. Paul reminds us of this when he speaks to pagans about "the living God, who made heaven and earth and sea and everything in them. In the past, he let all nations go their own way. Yet he has not left himself without testimony: He has shown kindness by giving you rain from heaven and crops in their seasons; he provides you with plenty of food and fills your hearts with joy" (Acts 14:15-17).

God is good to us all, Christian and non-Christian! And it isn't just food and clothing he gives to non-Christians; he gives them friends and health, beautiful babies and faithful husband and wives; character-filled parents and wise counselors. God is neither stingy nor sectarian. He loves the entire human race, and if there's anything beautiful or wise, heart-lifting or character-transforming in this wild world of ours, it's the generous gift of God. Israel's experience is a word to the entire world.

The appropriate response from all of us is a confession of our total dependence on and great indebtedness to God. The appropriate response from all of us is a trusting commitment of ourselves to God for victory over all the forces of evil and for a triumphant march home to glory, even though the way home is through the wilderness.

And of course, Moses had seen God's triumphant power in his own life, and this was why he could speak with such warm confidence to the Ishmaelite outsider, Hobab. Moses knew it wasn't just Canaan that belonged to God—the wilderness was just as surely God's. It wasn't simply that God was with Israel when they "found themselves in the desert." Moses knew that God *had deliberately and with purpose brought them into the wilderness,* and that's why he was with them in it.

But for all his genuine confidence in God, Moses had his moments of frustration and despondency. It's easy to imagine Satan, the World Hater, sidling up beside Moses when he was in one of those slumps and whispering, "How can you be so confident? Look where you are!"

Downhearted or not, Moses would have said, "Don't be so smug, we've been in worse places. We used to be in Egypt!"

"Perhaps, but look where's he's landed you; it's out of the frying pan and into the fire," the cynic might have said.

Moses might end the discussion with: "Egypt was more dangerous to us than this. If God got us out of there, he can get us out of here. Besides, I think you've forgotten we're on *his* mission and not our own. Stay till the end, and you'll see us crossing Jordan. God is with us."

Sometimes the wildness of this world leaves us breathless, and we wonder, "God can create a world, spread out a heaven, throw stars into limitless space the way people throw rice at a marriage, but can he take sinful people out of the wilderness, all the way home? Can he take the wilderness out of people and make them holy, through and through? Can he take us with all our weaknesses, all our entrenched sins and character flaws, with all our ignorance, and bring us to Canaan? Is he willing as well as able? Stars aren't inclined to disobey him, galaxies don't rise up in rebellion. It's one thing for him to succeed with elements that have no choice, but is that the same as dealing with humans, with our free will and our on-again-off-again longings? Can he see weak people like us safely home? Can he complete his overarching purpose through us?" Israel's wilderness experience is written to tell us, "Yes! Ten thousand times, yes!"

I'm one of those who thinks people can say no to God's offer of life and friendship. If we simply will not have it, we can "beat" God, but the eternal loss is ours. I don't have people like that in mind here. I have in mind those of us who long for better but can't seem to "get it right." I'm thinking of those of us who aren't even sure that we long for fullness of life with God but who long to long for it. We're in a fevered state because we don't want to miss it, and yet we see nothing in us but one form of God-denial or another. I'm thinking of those of us who don't believe we have to earn life with God but are always anxious in case there isn't in us a recognizable response of faith.

To these people I'm wanting to say: Our assurance that we'll make it home, that on the way we'll be blessed and strengthened even by the wilderness—our assurance if there is to be any, doesn't come from within ourselves. It doesn't come from our positive goodness or avoidance of evil; it comes because our God knows us completely and still works to bless us. We don't have to impress him, bribe him, grovel and crawl before him. He blesses us in spite of our sinfulness. If our assurance depended on performance rather than trust, if it depended on our virtue rather than on him, not only would we not have been called to his side, we'd never make it home.

Like Moses, we all have our times of weariness and frustration, and we hear the inner doubts and the outer criticisms. "Yes, yes, fine noble talk, but the stubborn fact is that the barren wilderness within you and around you is set against you!" We don't need to doubt this, but God is for us! Do you hear? God is for us! And the wilderness is his. The chaos is his. The heat, the glare, and the lifelessness around us are all his, and if it suits him to make us hungry and thirsty, so be it.

Moses knew of the difficulties facing God if he was to bring Israel home to the Promised Land. Didn't he rage against his own people when they built the golden calf? Hadn't he spent forty years roaming around the wilderness, taking care of Jethro's flocks? Hadn't he seen the challenges of living in the desert? Yes, but he'd seen more; he'd seen what God had done to Egypt and how the mountains had quaked at his very presence. Moses knew that God had used his almighty power on Israel's behalf because he had made promises to Abraham—promises God swore to keep.

All this enabled Moses to endure, and it explains the confident expectation in his words to Hobab. Moses expected one day to be done with the wilderness, done with barrenness, done with pitiless heat and water shortage, done with trackless desert, biting serpents, and choking dust. Done with a rebellious people. He spoke in eager tones about a land flowing with milk and honey, a land of streams and fruit trees, he spoke of home. And in the land of Moab as Moses says farewell to Israel as they were about to enter Canaan, his vibrant hope was justified.

So thoroughly did God tame the Sinai wilderness that centuries later, whenever Israel was in trouble, the prophets described its transformation as a way of calling Israel to look to God and to rejoice in hope of a rosy and assured future. Isaiah 35 is one perfect illustration from among many:

The desert and the parched land will be glad;
>   The wilderness will rejoice and blossom.
Like the crocus, it will burst in bloom;
>   it will rejoice greatly and shout for joy....
Water will gush forth in the wilderness
>   and streams in the desert.
The burning sand will become a pool,
>   the thirsty ground bubbling springs. (1-2,6-7)

With an abiding vision of God in their hearts, the Israelites not only saw beyond their great troubles to a better day, they also looked *at* their pain and saw glory. They gazed with expectant hearts at their present agony and saw it transformed into beauty. In the place of barrenness they found fruit, and in the place of a hot fevered soul, they discovered an assured, blessed life that was a blessing to others because God made them "a light for the Gentiles, that you may bring my salvation to the ends of the earth" (Isaiah 49:6). Before their very eyes Israel saw the threat to their life become the way to newer, richer life and to greater service for God.

Why must we go home through the wilderness? After we've said all we can say, there's no completely satisfying answer, but there's still God's insistent call for us to trust him to do all things well. Jesus called for this trust in his dealings with loyal John the Baptist.

Not many things test our faith more than God's doing all kinds of marvelous things for everyone around us while leaving us unblessed. Our cancer remains while others... Our babies die while others... Our marriages... Our children, our business, our parents, our health, our savings...while others...

When John the Baptist heard of the miracles worked by the Messiah, he must have felt neglected and a bit depressed. He sent two of his disciples to say to Christ, "Are you the one who was to come, or should we expect someone else?" (Luke 7:18). I don't think John doubts Jesus' identity (it was the miracles that provoked the visit); it's what Jesus *isn't* doing that troubles John.

Luke 7:21 says Jesus kept John's messengers waiting while he healed multitudes, before he sent the messengers back to John with a response. Imagine the messengers with wide eyes telling their master how Jesus freed a blind man from darkness, how he released a leper from his disease, how he liberated a woman from death. "The power God has given him to rescue people is beyond description," they might have said. But there's no word about freeing John, not a word about his release from the choking dungeon despite his great faithfulness.

When they told him what Christ said, John, bitterly disappointed, might have asked, "Yes, yes, but did he say anything about my getting out of here?" And they, assuring him that Jesus said nothing about it would add, "But he did say, 'Tell John, blessed is the person who isn't offended by me.' "[1]

John's in a personal wilderness, depressed and longing for better, longing for change, and the word comes, "Trust me! I'll take care of it all." John later got out of prison and went straight to glory, didn't he?

Trust always triumphs over the wilderness.

9

CELEBRATING THE
WRATH OF GOD

---

*Nothing is so sweet to the heart of man as love. However, for love
to function, the suppression of sympathy may be necessary.*

RABBI ABRAHAM HESCHEL[1]

Some people write and talk as though the only fitting response to
tragedy or suffering is a sagging of the shoulders, a broken whisper,
and a slow, painful walk. But in their desire to be compassionate,
these people spread weakness everywhere with the only song they
know—the dirge. They pour out rivers of sympathetic noises and dis-
able many in the process. They tell stories, you see, of people whose
hurt was dismissed as nothing, who were needlessly left to bear their
burdens alone—sufferers who then turned from God. And because
these well-intentioned storytellers don't want these circumstances
repeated, they go around spreading so much sensitivity that, compared with them, God is a brute.

So how do we look unflinchingly at the wilderness and say,
"Thank God for it"? James says it's possible! Experiencing the loss or
permanent maiming of our beloved doesn't generate the same feelings
as seeing a full recovery from a dread disease. And we're not to pretend

it does! One is agony and the other bliss. When James says we are to count it "pure joy" (1:2) when we experience trials, he isn't nurturing us in stupidity or nonsense.

We don't park our brains or our capacity to feel when we celebrate the wrath of God. To do this means we take a certain view of God. We're to think noble things of him, and we're to see him as unchangeably committed to humanity's ultimate blessing and salvation.

Cherishing this view of God, we're to respond gallantly to his severe mercy when it expresses itself in wrath. To respond gallantly won't mean we're made of stone, and we may well weep in anguish at our awful losses, but there are things we *will not* do. We won't join the peevish deserters who serve God as long as they see him as the best meal ticket in the universe. We won't become one with those who sneer, one of the abusive godless who rant and rave because their personal cherished dreams came to nothing. We won't take our seat with the scoffers or make other gods our lords.

It's possible to celebrate the wrath of God! The Israelites did it. One of their three annual feasts was the Feast of Tabernacles, which was not only an agricultural feast to thank God for (and pray for future) rain, it was also a celebration of those glorious but tough days in the wilderness when God protected and sustained them for forty years. For numerous reasons God's people were glad that the wilderness was a part of their past. And remember, it wasn't only those guilty of apostasy and unbelief who endured the pain and privation of the wilderness. Along with the guilty there were the guiltless whose hardship was vicarious, whose pain existed because they were part of a nation that was punished for its crass unbelief. The curse of the wilderness fell on the guiltless as well as the guilty.

"Yes," we're tempted to say, "but it's only when it's part of our past that we can celebrate the wilderness." This is often the case, but there are too many people—a countless stream of them down the years—who were able to rejoice in the Lord even while overwhelmed by trouble. Even if we aren't able at present to do the same, we can't, and don't want to, deny *their* glorious march through their wilderness. They stand brave and strong, sharing in the curse that God brought on all humanity when we rebelled in the garden. Others might snarl and scream at God with unbridled speech, but these sufferers bear their sorrow bravely, believing that a redemptive God is at work for the whole world. (I have no criticism of those whose suffering is severe and prolonged. We should hug these in silence rather than criticize.)

When James urged his readers to "consider it pure joy…whenever you face trials of many kinds" (1:2), he was telling us that under God even "curse" is blessing. James learned this from his master, who insisted that his people are blessed when they are persecuted for God's good purposes. Peter, too, told his readers to rejoice in their sufferings because it's for Christ's name that they suffer, and they are blessed because the spirit of glory and of God rests on them.[2]

Tens of thousands have told us that's how they felt when they came through their place and time of trial—they told us it was a time of joy. Some have even shown us—are showing us—how to rejoice when the blows are actually falling. We hear it from people as far away as Littleton, Colorado. We hear it from sweet Christians in Laotian prisons and from strong young lecturers in Belfast hospitals who can no longer speak because their cancered voice boxes have been removed.

Each of you knows the kind of people I mean. They're people like Linda who has Huntington's chorea. I met her last year in South

Dakota. I first noticed her in the assembly (how could I have missed her?) when I saw her arms flying up and down, in and out and across, in every direction. Her body was a ceaseless stream of involuntary jerks. Shoulders, face, head, arms, and hands all in movement, twitching and fiercely jerking; jerking so fiercely at times that it would turn her around in her seat.

I spoke to her afterward while she fed herself with surprisingly more success than I thought possible.

"It's going to kill me, you know," she said from behind the flailing arms and restless hands.

"And what do you think about God who has allowed this terrible thing to come on you?" I gently asked her.

"He gave me a gift," she shot back.

"Oh? And why would you say something like that?"

"It turned me around," she said. "I was going my own way with no thought for anyone, least of all him. It brought me to him, so I see it as a gift."

These are the kind of people G. K. Chesterton had in mind when he wrote his song of celebration in the face of redemptive wrath.

> *Though giant rain put out the sun,*
> *Here stand I for a sign.*
> *Though earth be filled with waters dark,*
> *My cup is filled with wine.*
> *Tell to the trembling priests that here*
> *Under the deluge rod,*
> *One nameless, tattered, broken man*
> *Stood up and drank to God.*

Sun has been where the rain is now,
Bees in the heat to hum,
Haply a humming maiden came,
Now let the deluge come:
Brown of aureole, green of garb,
Straight as a golden rod,
Drink to the throne of thunder now!
Drink to the wrath of God.
High in the wreck I held the cup,
I clutched my rusty sword,
I cocked my tattered feather
to the glory of the Lord.
Not undone were the heaven and earth,
This hollow world thrown up,
Before one man had stood up straight,
And drained it like a cup.[3]

The poet daringly looks right into the eye of God's storm and says, "Thank God for it!" The speaker has tasted God's goodness and kindness and is too committed to God to believe that his wrath is anything other than another face of his goodness. So he looks at a world that has been ripped hollow by the wrath of God, and instead of peevishly turning from God and cursing, he grabs the hollowed-out world, uses it for a cup, fills it with wine, and drinks to God.

God's anger is against *a world of people* so that he might redeem that world of people. The curse, which is his wrath made visible, embraces all humans: rebels and subjects, the innocent and the guilty. Should we drink to that wrath? What if it's part of his redeeming work? What if his wrath exists only to destroy what necessitates the wrath in the first place? What if we see it as a response from a holy Father who loves us beyond imagining? A Father who's willing to do more for us than we want him to do. A Father who does at a cosmic level what Annie Sullivan did to Helen Keller to rescue her from crippling, narrowing, cheapening blindness.

What if the suffering of righteous people and their sense of abandonment is part of the suffering and abandonment of Christ, who is yet suffering in and through his body, the church,[4] that the world might see and be redeemed? What if he who wouldn't spare his own unique Son, but delivered him up for us all, is doing the same thing with his sons and daughters in Christ? If we could believe that, if we could believe that somehow, in some way, in our loneliness and agony we are fighting God's battle for him against the forces of darkness and evil, that would make a difference in how we bear "the sore years."

While it's true that most of the suffering of God's people mentioned in the New Testament is persecution, it's not the only kind of suffering the writers know. Jesus, while preaching the good news of the kingdom of God, was "healing every disease and sickness among the people" and the "news about him spread all over Syria, and people brought to him all who were ill with various diseases…and he healed them" (Matthew 4:23-24). Matthew tells us he did all that "to fulfill what was spoken through the prophet Isaiah: 'He took up our infirmities and carried our diseases'" (8:17). In making use of Isaiah 53, Matthew makes it clear that disease and loss have come on humanity as part of the judgment of God, and Christ bore it on his heart for us.

In the meantime, as Rabbi Abraham Heschel has reminded us in his book *The Prophets,* "For all the terror that the wrath of God may bring upon man, the prophet [Habakkuk] is not crushed or shaken in his understanding and trust. What is divine is never weird."

We can't seem to get it into our heads that God has already and will again put the innocent and righteous to grief so that a sleeping world might wake up and live. The wrath of God that engulfed the innocent babies in Noah's day makes it clear that God is earnest enough in working for world redemption to do things that are distressing to him. Heschel remarks: "Nothing is so sweet to the heart of man as love. However, for love to function, the suppression of sympathy may be necessary."

We're not to think of God as unfeeling! We're not to give the impression that those who celebrate the wrath of God are unfeeling! It was God's full intention to bury Nineveh if she had not repented, but still the prophet Jonah went west to keep from carrying that message. And his excuse? When God decided not to ruin her, the angry prophet said, "O LORD, is this not what I said when I was still at home? That is why I was so quick to flee to Tarshish. I knew that you are a gracious and compassionate God, slow to anger and abounding in love, a God who relents from sending calamity" (Jonah 4:1-2).

Heschel insists: "An essential feature of God's anger as proclaimed by the prophets is its contingency and non-finality. There is no divine anger for anger's sake. It's meaning is...instrumental: to bring about repentance; its purpose and consummation is it own disappearance." God's wrath works itself out of a job. It was precisely because Jonah knew this about God and his wrath that he didn't want to preach to Nineveh. Graceless, loveless Jonah wanted Nineveh dead! Without chance of reprieve. A gracious God who loves the whole of humanity wanted her to turn and live.

The wrath of God is not a fundamental attribute of God; it's a passing and contingent reaction. He will turn from his wrath when conditions change, but he is everlastingly and unchangeably loving. Isaiah reminds us of this truth, "In a surge of anger I hid my face from you for a moment, but with everlasting kindness I will have compassion on you" (54:8). The psalmist adds his voice to the song, saying, "His anger lasts only a moment, but his favor lasts a lifetime" (Psalm 30:5), and, "The LORD is compassionate and gracious, slow to anger, abounding in love. He will not always accuse, nor will he harbor his anger forever" (103:8-9).

The wrath of God that has expressed itself in "the curse" will finally pass away when the last and bitterest expression of the curse—death itself—is swallowed up in glory. In the meantime, may God give us the grace and gallantry to celebrate his redeeming wrath.

10

Jesus' Blood Never Failed Me Yet

They looked toward the wilderness, and behold,
the glory of the LORD appeared in the cloud.

EXODUS 16:10 (NKJV)

Life's challenges can break our hearts and rob us of our dreams. I mean more than the calamities that befall us out of the blue or the devastating losses that rip away the foundations of our stable lives. I'm taking about the endless stream of low-level disappointments, like the job we didn't get, the promotion that went to someone else, the lovely person who didn't seem to know we existed, the nagging and hyper-critical parents or spouses, or our rotten kids who don't seem to have either a grateful or respectful bone in their bodies. Calamities are dangerous but no more dangerous, in the long run, than a weary slog through days that have lost their promise. Disaster can sweep us off our feet, but chronic sameness can suck us dry. I'm not sure who's worse off: the glassy-eyed plodder or the thunderstruck lying in a heap in the corner.

"Can anything good come out of Nazareth?" Nathaniel asked,[1] voicing our own depressed spirits. It was a gloomy and defeatist response when Philip's claim should have been eagerly checked out. Philip came saying the Messiah had appeared—the long-awaited Savior of Israel! But there'd been many messiahs who had proved to be fakes, and now here was Philip, staking his life and hopes on a northerner from despised Nazareth, of all places. Only hurt people, all twisted inside, could say in flat, toneless syllables, "Don't be silly. Nazareth? Have some sense."

Clashing armies, failed hopes, economic depression, political dead ends, quarreling religious leaders, bandits, civil unrest and false messiahs—this was the wilderness of first-century Palestine. Even good-hearted people like Nathaniel felt the life ebbing out of them. The desert was taking its toll.

And, humanly speaking, that's hardly surprising. Who needs to be convinced that the light can go out of our eyes, and that life's seemingly plotless story can beat us down? Exodus 6:9 tells us that when Moses brought a gospel of freedom to an enslaved Israel, they weren't able to hear it because of the bitterness of their spirits and their hard bondage.

The wilderness God brought Israel into was as bitter to them in some ways as the Egyptian bondage. Think about how the wilderness of Sinai must have seemed to them in contrast to the rich land of Goshen. The trackless, waterless desert filled with erratic boulders, twisted rock formations, panting reptiles in the shade of rocks, and stunted vegetation. Wouldn't their despondent hearts take note of the pitiless heat and changeless glare? Even good-hearted people would find it a place to endure rather than to enjoy. And if the people murmured insults, wouldn't they have reason to do so? "Would you look at this place?" they'd snarl. "This is *freedom?* This is better than Egypt?"

But while the wilderness never became the Hyatt Regency in Acapulco, God spread a table there for an entire nation and its flocks and herds. Isn't that amazing?

Had some wanderer gazed across this blistering desert, looking in the wrong direction, he'd have seen nothing but barrenness and ample reason for dismay. But if a fellow wanderer should come panting up to him to say, "There's a people living down there, a whole nation for pity's sake!" wouldn't he be tempted to dismiss the words as nonsense?

Yet if they'd made their way over a ridge and looked in the right direction, they'd have seen a whole people, their tents carefully organized around a grand central tent—visual harmony in the middle of chaos. And if they'd listened for only a moment, wouldn't they have been astonished to hear snatches of music and singing drift up with the wind? Wouldn't they have heard children laughing and seen people tending flocks and herds (yes!) and living as if they were oblivious to their surroundings? That's exactly what they would have seen and heard there in the awful wilderness!

And what do you suppose we're to learn from that? There before them and us is living proof that even in the heart of chaos, in the most threatening environment, life can thrive and flourish. The first question that'd jump to our minds would be, "How's that possible?" But what would generate the question would be amazement that the Israelites are alive at all! If someone were to say, "It's possible because God makes it possible!" that might be sufficient, but before we'd look for explanations, we'd rub our tired eyes one more time, just to make sure we weren't dreaming.

Our skepticism would be understandable because, humanly speaking, environment kills hope. It isn't surprising that psychiatrists, police, and social workers rank high on the lists of suicides, wrecked marriages, and the socially maladjusted. They ceaselessly work with dysfunctional humans in tragic situations, and this has a wrecking effect on their own lives and families. Work with con artists and liars, criminals and emotionally damaged and damaging people, day in and day out, and it isn't surprising that you wonder if anyone in the world is honest or well or genuine.

We see this even in Jesus Christ. He took the environment seriously and fully expected it to have its effect on people. Twice in the New Testament we're told he was amazed. A Roman centurion's great faith leads Jesus to marvel and say he hadn't seen faith like that in his very own nation (Luke 7:9). But why should Christ have marveled because a pagan outsider had such faith? *Because environment makes a difference.* And in the very same town, Capernaum, Jesus is astonished at the unbelief of his own people (Mark 6:6). Capernaum, a synagogue town, a town that prided itself on its Jewishness, was so hard of heart that Christ shook his head in disbelief. But why should Christ have been amazed?

All the paganism of a pagan world couldn't keep a robust faith from rooting itself in the heart of a war-hardened Roman veteran, and Christ loved it. All the rich heritage and history of the elect nation had failed to generate an open heart of faith, and this shocked Christ. He was astonished in both cases *because environment makes a difference!*

Israel in the wilderness teaches us that the God who created harmony in a chaotic wilderness can create harmony in the wilderness of the clashing nations of the world. Israel in the wilderness teaches us that God can make life flourish, can make faith burst out even in barren places. Israel in the wilderness says that if people give God even half a chance, he can manifest his sustaining glory in the worst of circumstances.

Even as you read this, you can think of people who were as far from God as you can imagine when, in desperation or in half a hope, they looked in God's direction and saw life rising out of the dust. Gavin Bryars tells of someone like that.

In 1993 Bryars produced an album called "Jesus' Blood Never Failed Me Yet." In 1971 Alan Power was making a film about people who were living rough around Waterloo Station, London. During the filming some of the street people would break into drunken song—sometimes bits of opera, sentimental ballads, or folk songs—and one tramp, who didn't drink, sang a religious song. Some of the footage wasn't used in the film and was given to Bryars, who worked his way through it until he came to the tramp singing, "Jesus' Blood Never Failed Me Yet."

Gavin confesses he couldn't share the old man's simple faith, but he found the song moving and the unaccompanied voice had something to it that led Bryars to think he could work it into a project he had in mind. His intention was to gradually add musical accompaniment to the old man's singing; a few strings, then more, then singers, and then perhaps a full orchestra. He took it to the Leicester Polytechnic to record the "looped" piece onto a continuous reel. When he got the process started, he left the room and went downstairs to get a cup of coffee, leaving the door of the recording studio open.

He says that when he came back, he found the people in the adjoining painting studio, a normally lively group, unnaturally subdued. "People," he said, "were moving about much more slowly than usual, and a few were sitting alone, quietly weeping." He goes on to say, "I was puzzled until I realized that the tape was still playing and that they had been overcome by the old man's unaccompanied singing."

This alerted him to the emotional power of the music and encouraged him to maintain the integrity of the tramp's singing and simple faith. The resultant album is Gavin's tribute to the old man (who died before he could hear what Bryars did), and it's a moving, rhythmic, repetitive, gentle testimony that can lay hold of a heart, making it brave and generous and strong.

It's more than that. The song is a lone voice that defiantly sings out into the darkness of wilderness. It's an old man's refusal to focus on the disappointments and hardships of a long life drawing to a close—a life that bears all the marks of failure, a life that could easily insinuate that nobody cared about him, *nobody*, no exceptions. It's testimony given by an old, "unremarkable" man that the wilderness isn't Lord; that the wilderness can lie!

We must see him, living in his cardboard box, day after day, night after bitterly cold night, and without the help of booze to dull his perception or the pain. It's hard not to let the imagination wander and think of this man reflecting on wasted years, weeping at times about friendships that lost their way and people who had drifted away from him. In light of all these sad possibilities, we need to hear him singing in his slightly tremulous voice laced with conviction:

> *Jesus' blood never failed me yet,*
> *Never failed me yet;*
> *Jesus' blood never failed me yet,*
> *This one thing I know,*

For he loved me so,
Jesus' blood never failed me yet.

I know and so do you that hosts of people lie down and die in despair when life becomes hard and goes on getting harder, or begins to narrow and grows suffocatingly narrower. I don't understand why multitudes go another way, but they do. They look at the wilderness, and it opens their eyes to the glory of God. It's there, where others can only see misery, that believers sense God's presence and sustaining grace.

Bryars's old tramp haunts me in that lovely way some people do. They keep us from having too high an opinion of ourselves, but they also enable us to believe that profound trust and gratitude is possible in the depths of the wilderness. Pleasure can lie, success can bamboozle, and money can blind, but so can wilderness.

I like to picture the camera crews packing up and heading off in the very early hours of the morning, home to their fine houses and their loving families, home to a soft bed and blessed rest while the old man makes himself "comfortable" under some used clothing for blankets, smiling a little and humming himself to sleep:

Jesus' blood never failed me yet,
Never failed me yet;
Jesus' blood never failed me yet,
This one thing I know,
For he loved me so,
Jesus' blood never failed me yet.

11

"MY GOD, MY GOD, WHY?"

The troubles of my heart have multiplied; free me from my anguish.
Look upon my affliction and my distress and take away all my sins.

PSALM 25:17-18

We all know what it is to be attacked by enemies of many kinds: illness, financial difficulties, social ostracism, despondency, loneliness, and personal sins. These enemies not only hurt and shame us, they imply that we don't love God (which is believable and frightening). Worse—and profoundly frightening—they imply that God doesn't love us. If our enemies can lead us to *really* believe that, we're damned without hope. They seem to have the facts on their side, and *that* sharpens the anguish and sense of loss in our lives.

This was just as true for the writers of the psalms as it is for us. The psalmists refused to look away or deny the harsh realities of life; they faced them with steady eyes. The truth is, they *insisted* on spelling out all their gouging doubts, disappointments, and pains. Even more startling, they did it in church!

The psalms aren't whispered conversations in side streets between huddled groups of apostate Jews. Israel sang them in the temple to God's glory and praise. Today we may read them and wrestle with them, but Israel offered them up as part of their communion with

God. These were hymns to God, not ultimatums like, "If you don't fix this, we're going to Molech or Baal!"

The psalmists often asked God for help against enemies who had the upper hand. We see this as well as anywhere in Psalm 22. The worshiper lays before God a weary protest about what's going on in his pain-filled life: "My God, my God, why have you forsaken me? Why are you so far from saving me, so far from the words of my groaning? O my God, I cry out by day, but you do not answer, by night, and am not silent" (verses 1-2). He can't sleep at night, he might be ill, and he seems to be fevered and sweating, then dehydrated. His joints hurt him, and he has lost so much weight that he can lie and count his bones as the moonlight beams through his window from the distant and silent heavens where God hides.

The psalmist knew about secondary causes and secondary agents, but he didn't want to talk to them or to bad luck. He didn't want to talk to the doormen, the outer-office secretaries, or even the inner-office private secretaries who shuffle theological papers. He wanted to talk to the managing director himself, so he burst into the office and said, "Why have you forsaken me?"

I think the director would tell him, "At least you've come to the right person. Under these circumstances, I'm glad you didn't let the others keep you from coming straight to me. They mean well, but they think they need to protect me. Have a seat, maybe I can help you."

And so the psalmist described his world: a place of wild bulls, of roaring, savage lions, and packs of wild dogs. He saw the ungodly people who stood in marked contrast to his own pitiful condition; he's a bag of bones and they are sleek, well fed, and prospering. Packs of cowardly dogs crept in to bite and wound, only to skulk away when he raised a feeble hand in his own defense. And when the kinfolk gathered, attracted by the news of his imminent death, they eyed the furniture and the other belongings, scheming to get their share, even tossing a coin to see who'll get what.

So, head in his hand—no, his heart in his hand—the sufferer wanted to know, "My God, my God, why have you abandoned me?" It isn't just the pain that mattered; he felt abandoned!

His jeering critics, who deny his love for God or God's love for him, add heartbreak to heartache. Won't anyone stand with him? Stand *for* him? Where do you go when, instead of counting bones, you count weeks and months and years, forgotten anniversaries, by-passed birthdays, special events and places? How do you stay alive? What keeps you from sinking without trace?

The psalmist triumphed through the stories of God's faithfulness told to him by significant others. Like every other nation, Israel sang her stories, and in her songs boys and girls learned their history as much as in other ways. In song the Israelites told stories of great deliverance—the kind found in the book of Judges. Stories of Gideon and Deborah, of Samson and Jephthah.[1]

These stories of God's grace were not only sung and written down, they were made part of a liturgical confession. When an individual brought his personal first-fruits offering, he gives it to the priest who lays it beside the altar and then hears the Israelite's confession:

> My father was a wandering Aramean, and he went
> down into Egypt with a few people and lived there and
> became a great nation.... But the Egyptians mistreated
> us and made us suffer, putting us to hard labor. Then

> we cried out to the LORD, the God of our fathers, and
> the LORD heard our voice and saw our misery.... So
> the LORD brought us out of Egypt with a mighty
> hand.... He brought us to this place and gave us this
> land... and now I bring the firstfruits of the soil that
> you, O LORD, have given me. (Deuteronomy 26:5-10)

Understand this, it isn't simply that the sufferer *knows* these stories, he's depending on them. They shape his view of God and tell him
that God is a savior of his people when they are in trouble, and so
these stories become the ground of his own hope for deliverance.
Agony and fear can swallow us up unless there's something that lies
deeper than our pain and panic. And for this pain-filled worshiper the
deeper reality is the character and faithfulness of God as seen in
Israel's hymns, narratives, and liturgy.

This is part of the power of nationwide stories; we're less inclined
to doubt their truth, even if our own personal story seems to conflict
with the others. The temptation is to pit our own experience against
that of many generations, but the ceaseless and massive witness of tens
of thousands helps us to keep our own experience in perspective.

So we need the biblical stories of God's faithfulness to get us
through the wilderness. We need to tell *those* stories, and we need to
tell of God's goodness and adequacy in our own personal experience.
Jesus says to the transformed man in Mark 5:19, "Go home to your
family and tell them how much the Lord has done for you, and how
he has had mercy on you." We need to tell our stories when we go out,
when we come in, when we lie down, and when we get up. Tell them
as we walk and as we rest. Tell them in the cozy nights at home and in

the busy days of bustle and noise. We need to tell them to our children with enthusiasm and warmth, with honesty but with confidence. "My feet had almost slipped, but then I remembered…"[2]

George Bancroft, known as the father of American history, illustrates well the power of stories to help us remember our roots and whose we are. He wrote a ten-volume history of the United States, which surveyed the period from the country's colonial foundations to its independence. He spoke of a prolonged period of bitter fighting between the newcomers and Native Americans that came to an end in one section of the country with both parties more than ready to talk.

They met on the bank of a river to speak of peace and the repatriation of the captive children from both sides. Some of the children had only recently been taken, and these were reunited with their families with little trouble. But a large contingent had been snatched in their infancy and had no way of knowing who their parents were. The years and the changes meant the anguished parents were unsure.

There they were, looking at each other, tempted to pretend, so great was their heartache, but there was no hint of recognition, no familiar features. Lonely parents and children standing over against one another, anxious to be recognized, more anxious about *not* being recognized. Then someone suggested that the mothers go among the children singing the songs they used to sing, retelling the stories they used to tell, or calling their children with the affectionate names of early days. They did, and children, with long-buried memories alive again, with tears of joy and faces lit up, ran and threw themselves into the arms of their longed-for parents.

What a stroke of genius! To rely on the power of stories to bring these children back from hell and restore to them the sense of belonging. Loving parents had laid a foundation of family experience that survived in memories buried deep in the soul. Living away from home, living under horrendous circumstances, living as strangers in a strange land with strange and distressing customs—wouldn't you think time and the agony of it all would have ripped away the mooring of their lives? But no, a story from home opened the floodgates and in rushed repressed feelings of security and happiness. Images of brighter, kinder days drove out the gloom of their most recent pain and generated hope for the future. Their stable, lovely world was restored when they recognized and embraced their parents. Stories of home, carefully deposited in open hearts, survived the onslaught of awful years and saved them from permanent loss. Can you imagine the lives of these children and parents if they had no shared narratives? Nothing to draw them back to each other?

What drew the prodigal back from the pigpen to his home wasn't the filth and degradation of the pen, but the warmth and dignity, the love and fellowship of his father. He didn't want to leave the pigpen and travel the world; he wanted to rise and go to his father! And it was the memories of home that defied all the squalor and riotous living of the more recent times. Nothing could rob him of the sense of his belonging elsewhere, nothing could rob him of the sense that he should be living above his present circumstances.

In Psalm 22 the sufferer recognizes that God was there even at his birth, looking after him. But he also claims that in his mother's womb he gave his heart to God. The songs his mother sang to him about the Lord, the stories she rehearsed about God's love of him, shown in part by her own love for him, sank deep into the psalmist's soul, and he couldn't get free of them, didn't want to be free of them. From that time forward, he was God's devoted servant and continued to be, even in the present chaos where life now found him.

With such an upbringing, it was more a question of how he could stop believing than of how he could continue to believe. Living in such a community and family like Timothy's,[3] is it surprising that the psalmist turned his face to God even when it appeared that God had turned his face from him?

But the glorious truth of Psalm 22 bursts the bounds of a single person and travels to the ends of the earth. It begins with an individual, moves to a multitude, continues with a whole nation, and ends with a whole humanity. The psalm surveys past ages and speaks of ages not yet born. Under the superintendence of the Holy Spirit, Israel sang this psalm of hope for all of us, for the whole world that God says he loves but appears to have abandoned.

The boldness and breadth of such a faith is a sight to behold in a world of believers who are frightened to think majestic things of God and too self-centered to think of anyone but themselves, "the elect." It's *humanity* God loves! It's as if the psalmist stands up and says to the whole wide world: "My God is the Lord of all, and if he has heard my prayer, he will hear yours also!"

Isn't this Christ's message when, bearing the suffering and sin of a world, he made Psalm 22 his own prayer? Fully identifying himself with a sinful Israel *and* a sinful humanity, he experienced abandonment at the hands of one who has made a loving commitment not only to his own Son, but to his child Israel *and* his beloved humanity. Just as the psalmist sensed that his experience was not only his own but that of all sufferers, doesn't Christ—the sinless one who gallantly stood with rebellious humanity on our side of a sin-created gulf—doesn't he express humanity's sense of abandonment as well as his own? I believe he did.

But even in his absence, God was present! In truth, wasn't it *through* being absent that God could be even more present, not only for Christ, but through him for countless others?

But how can God make himself even more near by staying away? Life is filled with illustrations of this truth, but John 11:1-44 opens the windows and lets the light in on it for us. Jesus had a number of close personal friends and Mary, Martha, and Lazarus, their brother, were among them. Lazarus becomes seriously ill and the sisters send for Christ, telling him "Lord, the one you love is sick."

Christ gets the message and says to his disciples that the end of the whole affair will not be death but glory to the Father and his Son. What follows is so surprising that John feels the need to repeat, "Jesus loved Martha and her sister and Lazarus." One would have thought that since Jesus loved them, he would have hurried off to Bethany to be with them, but that's not what happens. "Yet when he received the news that Lazarus was sick, he stayed where he was for two more days" (verse 6, TEV). Christ deliberately chose to stay away.

Lazarus dies without his dear friend's presence, and yet Jesus says, "I am glad I was not there" (verse 15). The end of Lazarus's sickness was not death but the glorification of God and his Son, and *that's why* Christ absented himself from the needy, sorrowing family two more days. That's why he risks their words of disappointment and mild rebuke. He chose to be absent so that Martha and others could see more clearly the glory of God and so that his disciples' trust in him could be deepened. Christ stays away so that his presence could be more strongly felt, his adequacy could be seen more clearly, and his Father's purposes would be accomplished.[4]

When the situation can't get any worse and you realize God cares, it deepens and perfects your faith. Only people who've been there know that. A God who can only help us when the sun's shining isn't big enough. When the awful storms come, God's keeping power is thoroughly tested.

But in the storms that rage across the earth, humanity itself is called into question. In William Styron's *Sophie's Choice,* the question is raised, "Where is God?" in the face of the unspeakable atrocities of the Nazi death camps, and one of the characters passionately wants to know, "Where is man?" If a humanity that is worthy of the name is to survive in a world like ours, it will only be found where God is shaping and sustaining it—and that's where wilderness people come in.

Wilderness people live on stories. They look at their own experiences and praise God for the richness of them. But when the pressure's on and their own tiny little lives seem to be telling a story of God's impotence or suggesting that God doesn't care, then wilderness people sing to each other. They sing old and new songs, songs sung by millions, and these stories stabilize the hearts of those whose feet are ready to slip. And when those in great danger have been saved, they add their stories to the grand chorus of praise, and here's the result:

> Posterity shall serve him;
> > men shall tell of the Lord to the coming
> > > generation,
> and proclaim his deliverance to a people yet unborn,
> > that he has wrought it. (Psalm 22:30-31, RSV)

12

A LITTLE BIT OF DEATH

I will fear no evil, for you are with me.

PSALM 23:4

Tom had loved Sarah ever since the first grade. How could he avoid it? Not only did she have gorgeous blue-green eyes, the kind you could dive into and swim forever, she obviously adored him. She wanted to talk to him, spent all her time with him, and told her secrets in big-eyed trust to him. He was destined to love her, so it was no surprise that they went through school together and then chose to attend the same college. They couldn't keep themselves from one another, and so no one was surprised when one day they announced they'd be married soon.

Their early years of marriage were joy filled. This pair who loved life took a dive into them, having a whale of a time. But then tough times rolled around—times when illness came calling and lack of money pressed them sore, yet nothing made a dent in their relationship. Sarah was fond of saying, "A little bit of trouble isn't going to harm two people like us!" and Tom would grin in pleasure as she said it. And she was right. If God ever made two people gifted with love for one another—a love that was tough and tender and deep and strong—if God ever made such people, he had made this couple.

Tom was fifty-five when they heard the devastating news. After a routine medical examination, the doctor told him he had cancer. At first they both simply looked at one another, stupefied. From there they moved to a pained denial. What would cancer be doing in a man like this? They had four thousand reasons why it couldn't be true—the doctor was wrong. A second opinion was needed and sought, but the second opinion only confirmed the original horror story.

After their initial shock, they quickly dived into medical and nutrition books. Their prayers became more fervent and frequent—also more specific. They were on an emotional roller coaster, confident that Tom would be all right and then fearful that he might not be; sure that God could heal him, but uncertain that God would want to heal him. But how could God say no? Too many people were praying for him—too many *good* people. Prayer warriors were devoting days and nights to imploring God to make Tom well. Letters and e-mails came from all over, assuring them that they were not forgotten, telling them stories of God's goodness. These were all friends of God, and surely God would take their heart's desire into account.

But Sarah and Tom knew their Bible, and they knew about many for whom anguished prayers arose, prayers that didn't bring what was wanted.

The weeks became months and matters grew worse. It became clear that Tom was sinking, and while there was no faith crisis—God was still God and God was still good—the tears were flowing. The nights were too long, but the mornings came too soon. Weariness and fear insinuated things they didn't believe, things they forcefully renounced—including disappointment with God. Still they believed that God was just and good, but when the awful waves of fear passed over her, Sarah couldn't dismiss the feeling that God was letting her down. No, he wasn't *wrong* but surely…

The hospital, the chemotherapy, the bruising regimen, the failed holistic medicine and nutritional drill, the same questions from a host of well-intentioned people, the sense of defeat while repeating again and again and again, "He's not getting any better, the doctors say." The failed prayers of the thousands of prayer warriors—it all took its toll.

Holding Tom's hand as he lay in his own bed, waiting for the approaching final day or hour, Sarah, unable to be brave, unable to comfort him or herself, having read all the verses, devoured all the articles, prayed all the prayers—she told him of her awful desolation. She talked of the already brutal sense of having lost him, of his going away and leaving her alone, without him. She tells him how unfair it is, how God has said yes to the prayers of others and why *couldn't* he grant this request? How would it interfere with an eternal purpose? An omnipotent God could work it into his plans, couldn't he?

And he, weak and feeling his helplessness, but feeling even more his overwhelming love for his sweet, lovely girl who had filled his life with so much joy, whispers his faith and hers. Faith in the God who not only gave his Son for the world, but who gave them to each other in love and honor and joy all those years ago. He reminded her of what she knew but needed to hear, that their deep love for each other was a part of the love God had for them both, so there could be no ultimate loss. "You believe that, don't you, my dear?" Weeping but with sturdy conviction in her words, she blurted out, "Oh yes! Oh, of *course* I do, Tom."

"Well," he said slowly, "if that's true, you don't think a little bit of death is going to harm two people like us, do you?"

She straightened up and was silent for a long time as she leaned back into the chair. Then taking his frail hand in hers, and with tears still flowing, she whispered, "You dear...lovely...man. Of course you're right. You're not going anywhere I can't find you, and I'll know you when I see you. A little bit of death isn't going to harm two people like us."

Wouldn't it be awful beyond expression if there was no one we could look to, no one we could trust, no one we could ask why? The Bible never treats death as a trivial matter. It always pictures it as an enemy.

It won't do to mouth glib words to grieving families about death's being nothing. It's true there are perfectly good grounds to help people who sorrow,[1] but that comfort was dearly bought and it's silly—sometimes utterly insensitive—to speak when silence is wiser. Better to hold the hurting people in sympathetic silence than babble on, even in soft tones, about death's being nothing. *Nothing* to those who are staring at the wreckage left in its wake?

Death is never simply a biological event, it always has a theological dimension. It speaks of human alienation from God. It speaks of the curse and implies a great death that lies like a covering over the planet. And I think people, for all their talk about not believing in God or purpose, sense this. Even many of those who fervently believe in God have a deep-down sense of disappointment and rejection when death fragments their home with appalling ruthlessness. Death's silent and soulless eyes insinuate that God has let us down, don't they? There's more to death than dying, and the world needs rescuing from it.

The death of someone in her eighties who has lived a full and vibrant life and is ready to give up her place among the living—that kind of death doesn't assault us the way the death of a child or a young mother or a murdered rape victim or a young father crushed at work does. The first we weep over, but the second raises unanswerable questions and generates explosive rage or dry-eyed deadness.

The expression "a little bit of death," has gently haunted me since I first heard it. The phrase has a ring that is gallant and not just brave. Its understatement implies that death is a terror, but a terror we won't give an inch to. There's a defiance in it that makes my heart beat a little faster as I think about it.

In the movie *Good Will Hunting,* Will finally tells his psychologist friend, Sean Maguire, about the terrible treatment he had endured from his foster father. When the father was about to beat him, he offered Will his choice of weapons by laying a belt, a stick, and a wrench out on the table. Maguire, who was no stranger to physical abuse, quickly assured Will that he would have chosen the belt—he thought it would have been the least painful. Will, with a grim satisfaction, said he always chose the wrench. When Maguire asked him why, he said it was an act of defiance, a refusal to grovel.

You think this is just a throwaway line in a silly movie? I *know* people who've lived their lives that way! I have a vivid memory of a boy held against the wall, being choked by his father until his face was turning black, a boy who was willing to die then and there before he'd say yes to the will of a brute. And if it hadn't been that someone arrived on the scene in the nick of time, there's not a doubt in my mind but that the boy would have slumped stone dead at the man's feet.

I think the film critic Michael Medved is right: More and more we're hearing people fret and whine at how hard their lives are. There's more pouting and petulance. But it's coming from those of us who have no real experience with hardship. Whimpering is a taught response. And while I think Medved is correct, we mustn't ignore the mesmerizing response to pain and deprivation of millions of gallant people around the world. I'm including homes that have no insulation against the loss of loved ones, no faith to sustain, no hope to help the sufferers in their sorrow and yet they go on with life. And if you wonder how they do it, if you wonder how people who aren't committed Christians live so gallantly, I'll tell you. Because God will not leave them utterly without help. Like Cyrus in Isaiah 45:1-5, they may not know they're being helped, they may have no commitment to God who helps them, but he has a commitment to them. It takes the God of the wilderness to overcome chaos and defeat devastation. And he does! In countless ways and through many people, people like Tom and Sarah, he breathes courage and cheerfulness into the lives of millions, some of them even know he's helping them and turn to give him thanks.

If you met Sarah today and asked her how things were since her husband's death, she'd tell you, "A little bit of death can't harm two people like Tom and me."

13

No Heavenly Sweetheart

He who did not spare his own Son…gave him up for us all.

ROMANS 8:32

A messenger rushed to Job's home with this news: "Your oxen were plowing, with the donkeys feeding beside them, when the Sabeans raided us, drove away the animals, and killed all the farmhands except me. I am the only one left."

While this messenger was still speaking, another arrived with more bad news: "The fire of God has fallen from heaven and burned up your sheep and all the herdsmen, and I alone have escaped to tell you."

Before this man finished, still another messenger rushed in: "Three bands of Chaldeans have driven off your camels and killed your servants, and I alone have escaped to tell you."

As he was still speaking, another arrived to say, "Your sons and daughters were feasting in their oldest

brother's home, when suddenly a mighty wind swept
in from the desert, and engulfed the house so that the
roof fell in on them and all are dead; and I alone
escaped to tell you."

Then Job stood up and tore his robe in grief and fell
down upon the ground before God. (Job 1:14-20, TLB)

Eliphaz tells him: "Is it any pleasure to the Almighty if you are righteous, or is it gain to him if you make your ways blameless?" (22:3, NRSV).

And then Elihu says: "Look at the heavens and see; observe the clouds, which are higher than you. If you have sinned, what do you accomplish against him? And if your transgressions are multiplied, what do you do to him? If you are righteous, what do you give to him; or what does he receive from your hand?" (35:5-7, NRSV).

What a thing to say to a man who's grappling for life in a wilderness! Here were these men coolly and deliberately spitting out theology, claiming that God doesn't care in the least how humans respond. Did the horrible thought cross Job's mind that it might be true? That maybe it wasn't that God was *unrighteous,* but maybe he was profoundly *indifferent* to human moral struggle? Was the human struggle for moral loveliness and spiritual integrity one big gigantic yawn to God?

No! That was a lie. A soul-destroying lie. A God-dishonoring lie. It was a lie then and it's a lie now.

Job wouldn't have been on the ash heap if his life had meant nothing to God. He wouldn't have been there had God not believed in him and been thoroughly pleased with him. No matter how things might look, God was proud of Job.

Imagine this scene between God and Job when the ordeal was over:

JOB: The way you treated me just lately made it
difficult at times to trust in you.

GOD: That's interesting, the way you treated me
earlier made it easy for me to trust in you.

We must take seriously the dialog between Satan and God in Job 1 and 2. Satan told God that Job was a hireling at best and a self-serving hypocrite at worst. God said that was a slanderous lie and went to Job's defense because he believed in him.

And he believes in *you*. Yes, you who sit nursing your breaking heart that's filled with questions and niggling doubts. You whose pain and anger sometimes spills over into speech that isn't right. You who, because your trouble has been around for years and your prayers for ease have gone unfulfilled, have emotionally given up (and yet here you are reading this)—he believes in you, too.

And if you hear a whisper from somewhere, suggesting in a sly voice, "Yes, but surely he believed in Job because he saw he was a great man. He can hardly feel that way about you and other lesser mortals," don't you believe it.

That's another lie. Push it from you.

The night they betrayed him, Christ's followers had been arguing among themselves about who was the greatest and who would have the place of prominence in heaven. Christ must have watched them with those big dark eyes of his, listening to it all. Then after teaching them, he tells them they are the ones who stood by him during his trials (Luke 22:28). How could he say that? How could he tell the truth and say that at the same time?

Were they embarrassed by the generosity of his heart? Did they look at each other and shake their heads in humbled unbelief? Were they ashamed of their own shabby thoughts? Did they feel awkward and want to protest that such a charitable assessment was too grand for them? "After what we've just been doing, you say that about us?"

Still he said it and said it sincerely. He said it because behind all their shortcomings, the disciples had given him their hearts and meant to be to him and for him all that they could be at that point. *And no one can give more than all they have!*

Yes, yes, this is fine talk geared for the people who *want* to believe it, but out in the *real world* isn't such noble talk without substance? Isn't it a flight from reality? Doesn't it ignore the stubborn facts of life?

Good grief, no! In every generation millions of people live this way. I'm married to one. Ethel, who has lived with chronic ill-health since she was six, has endured scores of surgeries, many of them major (including three open-heart operations). She has suffered cardiac arrest a number of times, experienced a couple of "mild" strokes, is diabetic, and has almost died on numerous occasions. As a result of a spinal bleed, she's paraplegic, and as the king of Siam would say, "Et cetera, et cetera, et cetera." In Ethel I see a life of brave and cheerful faith lived out before me day after day. And she's only one of multitudes.

We had a sustained period of stress not too long ago. I say *we* because Ethel's pain is my pain. You can't love as I love Ethel (as you love your own loved ones) without hurting when they hurt. In any case, there were endless infections. Three times we had to hospitalize her because they were threatening her life. She has a prosthetic heart valve that needs to be protected, and the antibiotics were creating intestinal tract chaos and endless accidents. The debris from these was eating up her skin, creating blisters, hacks, and raw flesh. She had spasms that came close to rigor mortis and that made it difficult for anyone to attend to her and keep the debris from getting back into her system. She was hot to touch, terribly swollen, and bone weary from all this and too little sleep.

It was tough on both of us, but one particular morning I told myself I was really going to do a great job today. I'd be cheerful as well as patient, prompt as well as competent. We have these little intercom boxes, and Ethel buzzes me when she needs me. I was up in the attic "hitting the books" when the buzz came. I almost floated down the stairs, effortlessly, got her bathed, changed, and settled and skipped back up again. Once more, the soft buzzer and the voice apologizing for disturbing me. No problem. Down the stairs. The well-practiced routine. Happy? Yes. Back up the stairs. Six or seven times later, the voice not daring to apologize, the descent, a bit more tension, the job done, a long look, no "are you happy?" before heading up to the study. After about a dozen trips, study was impossible. All I could do was wait for that rasping sound, that strident, snarling, jarring, demanding, traumatizing buzzer and the same tired, timid, "Jim?"

By this time I was thudding my way down the stairs instead of skipping. I dragged the door open and worked in silence, her tired eyes watching me, studying me, understanding me, being patient with me, longing to help me, forgiving me. Yes, especially forgiving me.

Only now her legs had gone rigid, they wouldn't cooperate; the junk was eating on her flesh and finding its way into her system. It *can't* be left. I was sweating with exertion, but her legs wouldn't cooperate and I couldn't take care of it. My frustration mounted. I stepped away from the bed with a look, silently asking this helpless woman to do something, even though I knew there was absolutely nothing she could do. I turned to the wall and yelled—a long, vehement protest, a lancing of a painful wound in my mind: "Aaaaaaaaaaaagh!" I turned back to the bed, wordlessly appealing, sweat running down my face, feeling I must be a doctor when I'm not a doctor, suffocating in helplessness, wanting to storm out of the room that was like a torture chamber for both of us.

She watched me in silence with a long steady gaze, feeling my pain, this poor, sick, worn-out girl. Then she began to move her arms as though she were marching and, glancing at her rigid legs that had defied my brute strength, she began to sing, "We shall not be moved!" to the tune of "We Shall Overcome."

That did it! I picked up a pillow and gave her a good beating. We laughed a bit, held each other awhile, and got back to work.

Stories like this are commonplace. It's hard to overestimate the wickedness, selfishness, and cowardice in the world, but it's easy to underestimate the gallant good that's there. There are brave, patient, cheerful people who by God's grace live that way because they believe God is counting on them to fight his fight for him against the forces of cynicism, darkness, and despair in this wilderness of a world.

But such bravery is really only savored when you have a breathing space. It's appealing as it flashes by on a movie screen or in verbal images where it's painless and mercifully brief. The cold hard fact is that God, who could put a stop to it with the breath of a thought, watches the suffering going on. Whatever else we say about a God like that, to endlessly croon romantic ballads about him as though he were a heavenly sweetheart is pathetic. Such a view of God not only ignores Scripture, it offends the millions who are beside themselves in pain or loneliness or in soul-crushing depression.

What would lead God to stand by and watch such suffering? If there *isn't* something of infinite importance going on, if there *isn't* something of profound, even eternal, significance going on in and through all this, is there not a good reason to protest against heaven?

God stands by because we have a need greater than unbroken happiness, greater than unending health and prosperity—we need redemption! We may smile and dismiss this as nothing, but God won't. We may rage and say that happiness at the social and physical level is all that matters, that come what may the body should be catered to. But God won't accept that.

Listen, it's never our body that's under attack; *it's our life before God.* In the war against sin and death, in the process of fulfilling his overarching and loving purpose for the whole of humanity, God reserves the right to express his steadfast love as he sees fit even if it means pain for his children. Understandably we don't like to hear this when suffering comes thundering at our door, but L. E. Maxwell was right:

> In the midst of mounting world misery and mystery…there are worse things than trouble, worse than pain, worse than death…. Thistles, thorns, sweat—better than sin. Sorrows, sickness, suffering—better than sin. Pain, poverty, affliction—better than sin. Wars, plagues, famines, disease, destruction, death—

better than sin. Endless tyranny, unpitied tears, broken
hearts—better than sin. *Ashes to ashes, dust to dust,* our
mortal coil destined to the invasion of a million
worms—*all better than sin!*[1]

God went to Job's defense, not to discover *if* Job would stand,
but to demonstrate that he *would.* And he left a record of it. A record
of a human in the darkness fighting God's fight for him against the
forces of darkness and at awful cost. The book of Job stands as a lasting witness that God can't always be depended on to act as we'd like
him to act.

And in our better moments we don't want him to be a heavenly
sweetheart. We want him to wage war, however he sees fit, against all
the wickedness within us and around us, and if that means we share
the pain of this world that is condemned and in need of rescue, we'll
take it on.

We've all met people who blaze with glory even in their trials.
They are burning bushes for God; they burn but they're not consumed. You know the kind I mean. God shows them suffering and
asks them to bear it. They walk around it, look it up and down, check
it out thoroughly, noting the sharpness and bitterness of it, fully aware
of the hurt and loss that it is. "Sure," they say to him. "Sure, I'll take
that on if you want me to."

And he who is no heavenly sweetheart glows with admiration and
takes note of it all.

14

I YIELD MY FLICKERING TORCH

I will stand at my watch and station myself on the ramparts;
I will look to see what he will say to me,
and what answer I am to give to this complaint.

HABAKKUK 2:1

George Matheson's whole world threatened to crumble when one he adored called off the wedding at the last minute. Devastated, he went home and wrote his justly famous hymn, "O Love That Will Not Let Me Go." In it he confesses his lack of understanding but gladly bows in trust to God's superior loving wisdom. He puts it this way:

> *O Light that followest all my way,*
> *I yield my flickering torch to thee,*
> *My heart restores its borrowed ray,*
> *That in thy sunshine's glow its day*
> *May brighter, fairer be.*

Matheson wasn't the only one who faced a world gone to pieces. It tormented the prophet Habakkuk that local warlords and gangsters were getting away with murder, so he asked God about it.

How long, O LORD, must I call for help,
>   but you do not listen?
Or cry out to you, "Violence!"
>   but you do not save?
Why do you make me look at injustice?
>   Why do you tolerate wrong?
Destruction and violence are before me;
>   there is strife, and conflict abounds.
Therefore the law is paralyzed,
>   and justice never prevails. (Habakkuk 1:2-4)

We would not have expected God's answer. He tells Habakkuk that he is going to right the wrong by swapping the local thugs for international thugs who are worse than the homegrown variety:

For I am going to do something in your days
>   that you would not believe,
>   even if you were told.
I am raising up the Babylonians,
>   that ruthless and impetuous people,
who sweep across the whole earth
>   to seize dwelling places not their own.
They are a feared and dreaded people;
>   they are a law to themselves
>   and promote their own honor. (verses 5-7)

Habakkuk doesn't think too much of this as an explanation, since it only made the problem more acute. So he presses God for more information. But while he's waiting, he tells us that he will do what he knows is right. He won't desert; he'll stand in his appointed place and wait.

God's Word comes as a promise that those who remain trustful will not be disappointed. Then the prophet, distressed to the core, gives us one of the most marvelous declarations of trust in the Bible. He yields his flickering torch to God:

> Though the fig tree does not bud
>> and there are no grapes on the vines,
> though the olive crop fails
>> and the fields produce no food,
> though there are no sheep in the pen
>> and no cattle in the stalls,
> yet I will rejoice in the LORD,
>> I will be joyful in God my Savior.
> The Sovereign LORD is my strength;
>> he makes my feet like the feet of a deer,
>> he enables me to go on the heights. (3:17-19)

Naive solutions can injure, but there's something that injures even more—giving the impression that God exists primarily to keep us from being hurt. A faith that has more in common with cotton candy than with the biblical witness creates not only the need for so many overly sweet explanations, it weakens our hearts and disables us.

While it's true that we don't have all the answers to the question of suffering, we do know what God has done in Christ, and Peter says if it's the will of God for us to suffer, so be it![1] If we're "gifted" with a difficult life as well as faith, we have God to thank (or blame) for it.

"For it has been granted to you on behalf of Christ not only to believe on him, but also to suffer for him, since you are going through the same struggle you saw I had, and now hear that I still have" (Philippians 1:29-30).[2]

The "health and wealth gospel" is untrue—every form and version of it, crass or subtle—and until we make up our minds to that, we'll be more tempted to crumble when heartache comes or tough decisions have to be made.

The pagan crowds at the Roman games expected to see Christians fed to the lions. *"Christianos ad leones,"* they'd yell. The second-century pastor and theologian Ignatius tells us that when the search for victims was conducted days or weeks before the spectacle, it wasn't uncommon for the "weakest boy in his quavering tones" to stand up and offer himself with, *"Christianus sum!"* Boys! Not waiting to be ferreted out, they stepped forward to identify themselves, "I am a Christian!" And every child who stood before that mob, petrified but trusting, could have said, "This is my body which is given for you!"

There was evil there at the Roman games, sinners were there, elements of chance and coincidence there—but God was also there, doing his will in and through all it all. To each child, each family, God came and offered a cup to drink, and each drank it. Say what we will about secondary agents and causes, say what we will about randomness and bad luck, say what we want about demonic powers and corrupted free will—say all that and more, but when we're through, say that God was there accomplishing his will. No helpless watcher, wondering what he could do to squeeze some good out of it—he was an active participant! He was offering up his children for a cruel world's salvation.

I think we rob these nameless children and their families of the glory that comes in service for God if we make their deaths nothing more than a senseless, brutal killing.

God was there in the deep darkness of Golgotha that awful Friday. A crowd of persecuted believers sent up this triumphant prayer of praise:

> When they heard this, they raised their voices together
> in prayer to God. "Sovereign Lord," they said, "you
> made the heaven and the earth and the sea, and
> everything in them. You spoke by the Holy Spirit
> through the mouth of your servant, our father David:
>
> " 'Why do the nations rage
>   and the peoples plot in vain?
> The kings of the earth take their stand
>   and the rulers gather together
> against the Lord
>   and against his Anointed One.'
>
> "Indeed Herod and Pontius Pilate met together with
> the Gentiles and the people of Israel in this city to
> conspire against your holy servant Jesus, whom you
> anointed. They did what your power and will had
> decided beforehand should happen." (Acts 4:24-28)

And when Pilate, Herod, and the rest gathered together to kill Christ, God was there, in and through them, loving and sacrificing his beloved for a human race, including the very people who hammered the nails and poured out the mocking slander. God became flesh in Jesus Christ and offered himself up, saying, "This is my body which is given for you." God didn't make himself present *after* Golgotha; he was present *in* it. It wasn't simply the murderers who took the life of the Christ, it was his Father taking his beloved Son to himself *by and through* the hands of wicked men.

And when Lori (who I mentioned in chapter 1) walked into the house and found her mother, Mary Chandler, brutally strangled, God was there! Mary, who'd lived her life for God, wasn't left alone with her murderer; no more than first-century children were; no more than Jesus Christ was. There are those who think bad luck and sinfully perverted free will fully explain Mary's death. No, it goes deeper than that. As she served God so freely and gladly in her living, I think she served him gladly in her dying. I think God gave her the cup, and she said, "Yes, Father!" In the same act, the murderer murdered his victim and God sacrificed a beloved daughter. I believe amid all the grief experienced in southern California in those days that this lady was silently saying, "This is my body which is given for you."

We don't like this cross business, but then why should we *like* it? But like it or not, it is our destiny. To servants who endured unjust beatings at the hands of harsh masters, Peter says, "To this you were called, because Christ suffered for you, leaving you an example, that you should follow in his steps" (1 Peter 2:21). You were called to this *because* Christ suffered for you and so left you an example that you should follow. "Called to this," he says. When suffering comes we aren't to think it a strange thing; we've been called to it! When a brutal master wrecks the faithful servant's jaw, what consolation does he have besides the truth that one day God will right all the wrongs? I believe we have the choice to believe that we are the servants of a redeeming God and so we can say, "This is my body which is given for you."

Of course it's true that Jesus Christ alone atones for sin by his death, but in carrying the message of reconciliation through the church, Christ continues to suffer for the world in the suffering of his people as they "fill up in [their bodies] what is still lacking in regard to Christ's afflictions" (Colossians 1:24). When people hurt the people of God, Christ continues to ask, "why are you persecuting me?" and when his people are afflicted, they *participate* in Christ's sufferings.[3]

You want to see the gospel exhibited before your eyes? Then see it as God lays down his life in the lives of countless children. See it as he lays down his life in Mary. See it as he continues to endure, in the new humanity of the risen Lord, the church, the opposition of sinful men, the scorn and brutality of a world he adores and has come to save. *This is the true and living God!*

If we can look at the murdered Christ and see the wrath of God against sin and his grace toward a world of sinners, why can't we see this in the death of others? The truth is, it isn't the biblical teaching that's difficult, it's just that the hurt leads us to question it. Pain and grief make it difficult, but it's not impossible. In trust we can yield our flickering torches.

British theologian P. T. Forsyth reminds us that God's power and godhood are not denied in his laying down his life to die in Christ— their truth and glory are revealed there. *Because* of his glory and power, he was able to lay aside the privileges of Godhood to be strangled on Golgotha. Pagan gods know nothing of this holy, loving hunger because they are no gods. "The cross is the overflow of exultant Godhead, its purple blossom,"[4] says Forsyth. The holy love of God drives him to Golgotha! It's the one unfakeable sign that God is actually present in the cross. Robert Browning puts it like this:

> *I think this is the authentic sign and seal*
> *Of Godship, that it ever waxes glad,*
> *And more glad, until gladness blossoms, bursts*
> *Into a rage to suffer for mankind,*
> *And recommence at sorrow.*[5]

If our God is a God like that, we can live without complete explanations; we can yield our flickering torches to him. Someone long ago had a dream that an evil being came to him claiming to be the true Christ. The dreamer was uncertain about the truth of the claims until he asked his visitor, "Show me the wounds." At that the evil one vanished.

God's love for his lost children is so holy, passionate, and enduring that he must suffer for them—and he does it in Jesus Christ and in his body, the church.

15

COMPETING WITH HORSES

*I don't know what else you'll get, but you'll get
hunger and cold and wounds and death.*

GIUSEPPE GARIBALDI

One of the most remarkable men in history is the prophet Jeremiah, who for nearly fifty pain-filled years tried to prevent his nation's headlong rush to self-destruction. His profoundly developed sensibilities and his circumstances combined to make his life a prolonged crucifixion. If ever a man lived in the wilderness, Jeremiah did.

From the moment he was called to be God's messenger, he was alone in a hostile world. The nobility was against him because he scolded their oppressive and luxury-loving hearts. Worse, the two sacred orders of which he was himself a part—the priests and the prophets—hated him. He was born at a time when these groups had reached their lowest point of degradation and corruption, and they were leading a willing nation to hell and exile. "An appalling and horrible thing has happened in the land: the prophets prophesy falsely, and the priests rule at their direction; my people love to have it so" (Jeremiah 5:30-31, RSV). He endured the hatred of the priests against a priest who had exposed them as gutless yes-men and the malice of the prophets against a prophet who had branded them liars and hirelings.

His own priestly village was a nest of conspirators, and even members of his family slyly undermined him.[1]

The Lord tells him: "Today I have made you a fortified city, an iron pillar and a bronze wall to stand against the whole land—against the kings of Judah, its officials, its priests and the people of the land" (1:18). The prophet was alone, a solitary voice, there was no one in reserve.[2]

Jeremiah is driven to distraction between what he has already seen and what God has told him he will see. A weeping, distraught, sensitive human being, he wishes to high heaven that he could run away to a solitary shack in the desert so that he wouldn't have to see either his people's corruption or their crucifixion.[3]

> The Time is out of joint; O cursed spite,
> That ever I was born to set it right.[4]

Jeremiah curses the day of his birth, wishes he had been stillborn, laments his loneliness without a wife, and the isolation he suffers because no one wants him around.[5] In times of deep frustration, he turns on God and bluntly accuses him of betrayal and callousness. "O LORD, you deceived me, and I was deceived; you overpowered me and prevailed. I am ridiculed all day long; everyone mocks me" (20:7).[6]

Jeremiah hates the one-string message he's been called to preach. Year after year he tells Israel that judgment's coming, and then people mock him because it doesn't—this galls him. He wants to quit preaching and go back to ordinary life, but as he walks the streets and sees the evil, he can't keep his mouth shut.[7] Year after year he sees the Israelites' corruption and lives in pain, knowing what's ahead.

At times, goaded beyond measure by the people he wanted to save, Jeremiah becomes angry when God seems slow to judge them,[8] and in a fit of pain, he urges God to get on with it.[9] But when the judgments begin, one wave after another, he's in agony at the cries and the sights.

This is Jeremiah's life! "Of all the martyrdoms of the Bible—and it is a long record of martyrdoms—there is none so unrelieved as this one," said Scottish preacher Hugh Black.[10]

It's hardly surprising that at times Jeremiah beats on God's chest, telling him that he's tired of this kind of life, tired of its disappointments, its loneliness. He's tired of standing alone, tired of being friendless, tired of seeing others happily married with healthy, laughing children, tired of worrying over what spying people are saying about him, tired of watching from the shadows while others are giggling and enjoying themselves. He's worn out by the same gloomy message that has no gospel in it, worn out by savage ingrates and the I've-no-time-to-listen-to-doom people who can't see that he's slaving for *them.* Jeremiah's fed up with a God who insists on putting him through all this.

Given his wilderness life, it's no surprise to hear Jeremiah sob as he rocks back and forward in pain:

> Oh, that my head were a spring of water
> > and my eyes a fountain of tears!
> I would weep day and night
> > for the slain of my people.
> Oh, that I had in the desert
> > a lodging place for travelers,
> so that I might leave my people
> > and go away from them. (9:1-2)

Haven't we heard people who, when seemingly about to be crushed by a life that's too noisy or too quiet, too painful, too demanding, seemingly pointless, every morning coming too soon and every night lasting too long—haven't we heard them cry out to God, "Let me out! Let me out! For pity's sake, let me out! Is that asking too much?"

If you were God and one of these people came to you, tears flowing and heart breaking, wouldn't you feel bound to take him in your arms and console him? Wouldn't you, with all the power in the universe, jump right up and bury the villains who were hurting him? Wouldn't you right the wrongs, paralyze the oppressors, and deliver your faithful servant, your own child?

Perhaps. But what if you also loved the people who were causing your child's distress? What if you needed someone to live with them, sharing their pain? What if you *couldn't* just let the others vanish without trace, and so you needed someone to plead with them? What if you so loved them *all* that you felt compelled to send your child—a child you dearly loved—to redeem them *or* to leave the record of a tragic but wonderful story of costly love rejected so that future generations would listen, be moved, and be redeemed?

That'd be hard to do, but Christ was up to it, and so he said to his friends, "I send you out as lambs among wolves" (Luke 10:3, NKJV). And just that surely, God is up to it; God has the character, strength and love enough for *all* to do it.

When Jeremiah wants to know why the wicked are still prospering after all his preaching about judgment, God replies, "If you have raced with men on foot and they have worn you out, how can you compete with horses?" (Jeremiah 12:5).

Isn't this cruel? Why does God speak this way to an abused person? Does he think that just because he's stronger than all of us, he can say or do anything he wants?

Some might think so, but maybe those aren't the right questions. Maybe we should begin with the truth that God loves Jeremiah, and of all the people in the world, he has given Jeremiah the most important job in the world. What a faith God had in this man that he gave him such a responsibility, and what love he had for him that he wouldn't let him off the hook. Had Jeremiah packed his bags and run off to a deserted place, he himself would have been forever disappointed in himself. God's words to him weren't cruel, they were to make him strong so he'd see the job accomplished.

When Giuseppe Garibaldi took his one thousand "Red Shirts" (soldiers who'd already been involved in one battle after another) to fight for the unification of Italy, they wanted to know what they'd get for all their troubles. He told them, "Well, I don't know what else you'll get, but you'll get hunger and cold and wounds and death. How do you like it?" They stood silently for a moment and then threw up their arms crying, "We are the men! We are the men!" and off they went to war.

God's purpose for humanity is true and pure and eternal. God calls into active, costly service the people he loves. They aren't cannon fodder or dispensable items. The sacrifices are his when he sends his people to serve the unlovely. We aren't to interpret God's loving ruthlessness as cruelty, because he's after a whole world—a big, round, teeming, dying world—to redeem it. God sees sinners who are being driven into the darkness by the World Hater, and as he said to Jeremiah and countless others: "Come, I have a task of wondrous proportions for you. Among the things you'll get for your trouble is…"

In the tens of millions, down through the centuries they threw up their arms and cried, "We are the women! We are the men! We are the children!"

16

HOPEFUL PILGRIMS

They went about…destitute, persecuted and mistreated—
the world was not worthy of them.

HEBREWS 11:37-38

Princeton philosopher Walter Kaufmann believed that life became less exciting as soon as you thought you had endless existence. He said that if you knew you were going to die at forty, you'd live your life with greater urgency and intensity. I think he had a point, but it's not the brevity of life that gives it worth.

This much is true: Life that's a listless, frittering away of time and opportunity, life with all the risk and adventure removed makes a poor substitute for involvement, for really living. It's good to believe in life after death as long as we believe in life before death.

Humans have such a capacity for adventure and life that squandering one's life is only another form of death. This has implications on our views of life after death. Heaven can hardly be floating around on a cloud, bored witless, beating the brains out of a harp. Future life that will be better than life's best now must be *life.*

Life and literature are filled with examples of those who frittered life away and also those who lived life to the hilt. Both of these responses are well illustrated in Homer's story of the lotus-eaters.

Odysseus and his crew arrived at the island of the lotus-eaters, where the people fed on the seeds of a lotus plant that drained them of all desire to do anything but lie around. Some of the crew ate the seeds and promptly dismissed their homes and families. They had fought the gods and the seas, the monsters and the elements—never more alive than then. Now they didn't want to exert themselves. Their one desire was to lie around, looking forward to their next meal of lotus seeds. For a while they forgot they were pilgrims.

In the novel *Watership Down,* Hazel and a company of pilgrim rabbits, heading for a new home, meet a warren of rabbits who talk only of dying. They exist like zombies on human handouts. The pilgrims are horrified because there's the smell of doom in the air, an embracing of death, so Hazel and her group run—for life. It's a disturbing image that has more to do with people than with rabbits.

Author Lois Cheney tells of people who strenuously avoid the challenges of life; they can't be bothered with the involvement, grime, and inconvenience. When they die they come to God and say, "Here's my life," and God dryly asks, "What life?" He takes a dim view of our wimping our days away and calling it life, of our settling for less because it's too much trouble to stretch for more. Jesus Christ came not only to convict us of our crass sins, says Harry Emerson Fosdick, but to convince us of our possibilities!

Full of the love of life, the poet Robert Browning insisted that we're to look for all that life has to offer, refusing a blindfold at any time, living right to the brink and "earning" our death. I'm sure he's right, even though that's incredibly difficult for some. But according to Hebrews 11 there are pilgrim people who did it.

All these people were still living by faith when they died. They did not receive the things promised; they only saw them and welcomed them from a distance. And they admitted that they were aliens and strangers on earth. People who say such things show that they are looking for a country of their own. If they had been thinking of the country they had left, they would have had opportunity to return. Instead, they were longing for a better country—a heavenly one. Therefore God is not ashamed to be called their God, for he has prepared a city for them. (Hebrews 11:13-16)

God's people, richly blessed with their story and their place in God's purpose, have good reason to be gallant and hopeful. We know that this tough, sometimes agonizing trek on earth is but a "going home" experience.

The English poet and novelist John Masefield catches the Christian's pilgrim status in his poem, "The Seekers."

Friends and loves we have none
Nor wealth nor blessed abode,
But the hope of the city of God
At the other end of the road.

. . . .

Only the road and the dawn,
The sun, the wind, and the rain,
And the watch fire under the stars,
And sleep, and the road again.

We travel the dusty road
Till the light of the day is dim,
And sunset shows us spires
Away on the world's rim.[1]

We know we're going to die, of course, but we don't take seriously that we're pilgrims on this earth, so we don't travel light, the way pilgrims are supposed to do. We don't know how to travel light. We burden ourselves down with "things" and innumerable obligations. These sap our energy and we fall by the wayside of life. I suppose it need not be so—it certainly *shouldn't* be so—but having a host of things or clinging relationships makes it hard when Christ says, "Sell all you have...then come and follow me" (Mark 10:21, TEV).

But thousands can testify that liberation came when they lost so much of what they thought they had to have and were driven by a single, master purpose.

Christ met a man named Levi, secure in his job as a tax collector, raking it in and not thinking of making a change. The Master spoke to him, and Matthew tore down his whole world and set off on a quest finally alive.

Robert Louis Stevenson announced, "Our business in this world is not to succeed, but to continue to fail in good spirits." He went on to say about a friend: "The tale of this great failure is, to those who remained true to him, the tale of a success. In his youth he took thought for no one but himself; when he came ashore again, his whole armada lost, he seemed to think of none but others.... He had gone to ruin with a kind of kingly abandon, like one who condescended; but once ruined, with the lights all out, he fought as for a kingdom."[2]

Make of it what you will, but something about a major loss sharpens our focus and maximizes our energy for important tasks. If we're servants to ten thousand competing little loyalties, an experience that clears those loyalties away is a deliverance, however painful at first. Dithering between two thousand visions—or two—weakens us. But what if we made up our minds that we should count everything loss for the sake of Christ, as the apostle Paul did? Maybe life would become adventurous and hope-filled, maybe the "same old world" would be shot through with glory.

Hopeful pilgrims don't see life in the way others do. In *Pilgrim's Progress,* when Christian and Faithful entered Vanity Fair on their way to the Heavenly Jerusalem, the people became angry with them. The two were different, you see. They didn't dress like others, their speech wasn't like others and they weren't in the least interested in the items for sale at the fair. So when one merchant mocked them and said, "What will you buy?" the strange pair replied, "We'll buy the truth."

That response may sound a bit overly pious to our twenty-first century, politically correct ears, but it has the tone we find in much of the biblical witness. We may be able to use the political process to get our rights, but why should we expect the world to admire and cater to us? Perhaps we should be worried if and when it does, and perhaps we should feel even worse when we damn it and at the same time call on it to secure our rights by force of arms or economic sanctions.

So much of life is shaped by the way we see things; it's a question of vision, don't you think? Some of us moan from morn till night, and others couldn't be bribed into whining. Some of us can't face a situation without thinking the worst is bound to happen; we're all gloom and doom, while others see a challenge and glorious possibilities in the same situation. Maybe that's because people like myself keep speaking the same truths in the same tired old way, and people become as bored with them as the speakers and writers do.

I'm not suggesting there aren't unchangeable truths; everything is *not* up for grabs. But it's an awful state of affairs when, in practice at least, we've stopped looking for new truth, for a new way of looking at God's way with the world. J. S. Stewart said this better than I can:

> This is what God intends His Church to be—not a static camp, but a marching army; not the arrested development of an introverted fellowship which, having a certain amount of religious tradition in the background, blindly imagines that there is nothing more to find and no more land to be possessed—as though Christ's were "the touch of a vanished hand, and the sound of a voice that is still"; not that—but a host on pilgrimage, with the certainty, the glorious humbling certainty, that they are only on the edge and outskirts of God's immeasurable grace, and that always there are new insights to achieve, new wonders to explore, new depths of the unsearchable riches to fathom.[3]

Yes! However we work out our pilgrim status under God and in this world, we're not to anguish as though what happens in this life is the last word. We're not to pretend we're already "home." Those who are God's claim they've been liberated and are on the march. They claim that their progress through this world is a sign that God is at their head and center. They claim they are a colony of heaven, ordering their lives to please the emperor across the sea who is one day returning to complete his glorious work. And they insist that whatever the wilderness holds for them, God is in it with them, so they'll see it through in good spirits.

Edith Banfield saw a lot of this in her experience. It filled her with a warm sense of pride that she was part of a world that contained such people so she wrote:

> *This do I glory in beneath the sun*
> *That men have lived brave lives in evil times*
> *Have kept glad-hearted under stress of pain*
> *Have fought against all odds, and not despaired*
> *Have fallen and died exulting. So may I*
> *Keep an undaunted spirit all my days*
> *Lose not the larger view, hold fast the joy*
> *And with high courage come unto my grave.*

William Barclay, the widely read Scots commentator, was speaking of Abraham and others who are listed in Hebrews 11 when he said, "Above all things, God is the God of the gallant adventurer. God loves the man who is ready to venture for His name. The prudent, cautious, comfort-loving man is the very opposite of God. The man who goes out into the unknown and who keeps going on will in the end arrive at God."[4]

Yes, God is with us at the end, beginning, and middle of our pilgrimage on this earth. Remember, there's a difference between pilgrims and wanderers.[5] Pilgrims are going somewhere; they have a goal and purpose, and however difficult the trek might prove to be, they're going home.

Winifred Holtby was a brilliant Oxford scholar, an author and lovely character who died tragically at age thirty-seven. She wasn't a Christian, but in one of her letters to a friend she says that she was present at a dedication service for a fellow student who was going to China as a missionary. Holtby observed:

> It must be nice to decide to dedicate oneself to one
> particular form of service as she did when she was
> about twelve, and then train, prepare, and go and do
> it. And on your going, to have eight hundred people
> to pray over you and say that you do right. There is a
> satisfactory definiteness and conviction there about
> things.[6]

Then she adds wistfully:

> The difficulty is to what one can dedicate oneself. I
> am blown about by a wandering wind of great pity
> and sorrow and desire, while my weakness and self-
> indulgence and timidity keep me tied to the earth.

Now that's pain! Tied to the earth by timidity and self-indulgence. Holtby wasn't alone in her sadness, was she? Many of us know exactly how she felt. But God is good; he will deliver us and defy the world's

gloomy images and weakening power, and when he does, we'll sing
John Bunyan's song of the pilgrim:

> *Who so beset him round*
> *With dismal stories,*
> *Do but themselves confound—*
> *His strength the more is.*
> *No foes shall stay his might,*
> *Though he with giants fight:*
> *He will make good his right*
> *To be a pilgrim.*[7]

17

LIFE ON THE ASH HEAP

For your sake we face death all day long;
we are considered as sheep to be slaughtered.

PSALM 44:22

Loving trust triumphs over suffering. Simply by its existence, it defies the death-working power of the wilderness. In the face of the wilderness's blunt and harsh message, loving trust says: "I don't believe you! You can make me cry, you can frustrate me, and at times even make me scream in protest in God's face, but you really serve his purposes and mine. I've outgrown you, triumphed over you, and through the pressure you've put me under, I've been so strengthened that I can outwrestle and outlast you.

"I used to think you could make me do anything, betray anyone, give up on everything. I was wrong, and God has used you to make that clear to me. I couldn't have known that without your confronting me. I couldn't be what I am today without your opposition. You worked to destroy me, but all you've managed to do is make me stronger. People like me are spreading the word about you. You're a bully and a bearer of gloom, but we're seeing through you. The God we serve, the God who loves and enriches us, makes use of you and then dismisses you. You're pathetic!"

The story of Job not only shows us that God is no heavenly sweetheart, it also thoroughly exposes the limitations of the wilderness as a bully. While Job was rich and generous and upright and living in a big house, he was a thorn in Satan's eye as every good man and woman is. But the bankrupt, diseased, lonely Job who scraped the maggots from his flesh in between his groans and screams against heaven—that Job drove Satan crazy.

"He grovels before you," Satan told God, and then heard the man fiercely challenge God to a duel. "Take away his blessings and he'll walk away from you," the cynic said. But it must have broken Satan's heart when he discovered that Job had no intention of walking away from God. In fact the battered Job wouldn't let God walk away.

Someone should have taken the ashes of Job's ash heap and put them in a great big jar and made a memorial to the little man who made it clear to all the world that humans can stick with God when even God himself is making it difficult for them. Job's triumph is the triumph of us all: His triumphant trust says that by God's grace humans are up to the task. He reminds us that humans in the tens of millions are trusting God in the wilderness. Job's triumph says that wilderness life is not only bearable, it deepens with every tough, demanding day.

In *The Interpreter's Bible,* Paul Scherer comments on Job's wilderness experience with this quote from James McKechnie:

> It is not enough to say that [Satan] loses in spite of his gains—that does not express the full irony of his position—for, indeed, he loses by and through his gains. He makes Job a rebel, and in rebellion he lays grip on

a deeper loyalty. He provokes him into complaints against God, yet these complaints mark not a renunciation of, but agonizing struggles after God. He makes him a heretic, a passionate repudiator of the faith of his people, yet even while the old faith is being destroyed, a new and nobler faith is taking root in his heart. Satan is thus, in most unforeseeable fashion, duped by his own activities.… Never by way of natural and necessary sequence does good come out of evil. It is as a glad surprise, a miracle and triumph of grace, that it comes. Satan accomplishes nothing for God, though God may accomplish much through Satan.[1]

When he needs to be, when it suits his strong, holy, and loving purposes, God can be ruthless. Job might have been willing to just ignore Satan's opinion rather than have God wager on him at such a cost. It isn't hard to imagine this exchange between God and Job when the storm had subsided:

> GOD: Something happened behind the scenes that you weren't to know.
>
> JOB: You shouldn't have punished me!
>
> GOD: I didn't punish you. You didn't do anything wrong.
>
> JOB: Then you shouldn't have cursed me!
>
> GOD: I didn't curse you; I blessed you.

JOB: You call this blessing?

GOD: You were slandered, and I went to your defense.

JOB: You call attacking my body "defending" me?

GOD: It wasn't your body that was under attack—it was your integrity, your relationship with me!

JOB: Your putting me to grief made even my friends doubt my integrity.

GOD: I know, but we both know they were wrong.

JOB: They wouldn't have doubted my integrity if you hadn't put me to grief.

GOD: They could never have been sure of your integrity—or their own—if I hadn't put you to grief. I was betting on you!

JOB: Your betting on me cost me a lot.

GOD: Yes, that's very often the case. But the drama isn't finished until it's finished.

JOB: Because of my pain, your silence, and their words, I got to thinking you were punishing me because you thought I was bad, because you were disappointed in me.

GOD: No, I put you on the ash heap because I knew you wouldn't disappoint me. I put you to grief

not because you were bad but because you were
good. You can't know how proud I am of you.

Somewhere in all this, as we watch brave lives and reflect on the biblical witness, we're going to learn that life on the ash heap is just as surely life with God as is life in the sunshine. After all, was Christ ever more alive than when on the cross between two sinners? Was Paul ever more alive than when God was having to cancel the death sentences he received? Here's what he said in 2 Corinthians 1:8-9: "We were under great pressure, far beyond our ability to endure, so that we despaired even of life. Indeed, in our hearts we felt the sentence of death. But this happened that we might not rely on ourselves but on God, who raises the dead."

What happened at Job's house happens all over the world in every generation. It's happening in your generation and in mine—or it will. In a special way and at a special time, there will come a crisis when each of us will stand speechless at our loss and someone will whisper, "God couldn't care less," but we'll know the crisis will pass and there will be a happy ending. In the meantime we'll continue to fight God's battle for him against the forces of evil and cynicism, thrilled at the thought that we're part of a privileged company.

18

In the End — God

God is our refuge and strength,
an ever-present help in trouble.

PSALM 46:1

A young man, proclaimed by God as one of his children, fresh out of Egypt, turns to look at the wilderness that now faces him. He feels the scorching heat flowing his way, sees the trackless expanse of sand and rocks stretching out before him and merging with the horizon. The stories he had heard over and over again said they were leaving Egypt to go to a land flowing with milk and honey, and now, assaulting his senses, this shimmering, ominously silent specter waits to swallow them up. Dismay wells up in him.

Just a tiny human, he's vulnerable in a thousand ways; his heart can be broken, his body mangled, and his well-ordered internal world can be turned to shambles without warning. How can he face this…this…brooding menace, soon to be more than a threat? How can someone as puny as he possibly triumph in a place like this? Isn't despair the inevitable response?

"Look at this," he calls to some friends, and they join him in a long, pale-faced silence. But then, in a moment of splendor, remembering that God had rescued them from a long and bitter bondage, one young woman begins to sing, "God is our refuge and strength, an ever-present help in trouble. Therefore we will not fear, though the earth give way and the mountains fall into the heart of the sea" (Psalm 46:1-2). The Israelites had just seen the Lord tearing the Red Sea apart and buckling the earth with mighty winds. If their God can handle all that, he can bring them through whatever lies ahead.

Taking their cue from her, others join her, scores and then hundreds. Before we know it, a whole nation stands looking steadily at their enemy and singing their defiance in God's name. Many of the voices quiver with anxiety, and the strength of their emotions can't match the strength of their conviction, but they sing of God's power and willingness to see them home. *This is the Christian's appropriate response to wilderness!* The wilderness is a harsh reality, but it's not the ultimate reality. *God* is the ultimate reality, and the wilderness is his.

Another follower of God, fresh out of captivity to Lord Sin and with thoughts of a whole new creation as her inheritance, turns her eyes eastward to where the sun rises to banish darkness, and there sees chaos. Her mind reels and her heart flutters because she recognizes brutal realities for what they are and because the glorious promises seem now to be just so much talk by word merchants. But as she anxiously muses, she realizes that by God's grace she has a choice. She can allow the sorrows and gouging disappointments of life to swallow her up, or she can focus on the reality of God as he has shown himself in the crucified Lord Jesus Christ. The Lord Christ is just as real as bone cancer, just as real as clinging sin, just as real as depression and paralyzing fear. *God* is the ultimate reality, and the wilderness is his.

Scripture tells us that the wilderness is the work of a holy Father pursuing a holy and loving purpose. Contrast that glorious purpose with the deadness of one offered by unbelief. In his 1902 essay, "A Free Man's Worship," thirty-year-old atheist Bertrand Russell paints a grim picture of the present and thus of the future. He reworks *Doctor Faustus* and has Mephistopheles tell the doctor that God was bored with angelic worship, so for amusement he created the world and humans, made life as difficult as possible, and watched to see what they would do. When the humans bravely but stupidly try to make sense of it all, and even give thanks to God for his goodness, God, who has seen enough, sends a sun to smash the earth, ending it all. "Yes, it was a good play," God murmurs. "I will have it performed again." Russell goes on to say:

> Such, in outline, but even more purposeless, more
> void of meaning, is the world which Science presents
> for our belief…man is the product of causes which has
> no prevision of the end they were achieving…his ori-
> gin, his growth, his hopes and fears, his loves and
> beliefs, are but the outcome of accidental collocations
> of atoms…no intensity of thought and feeling, can
> preserve an individual life beyond the grave;…all the
> labor of the ages, all the devotion, all the inspiration,
> all the noonday brightness of human genius, are des-
> tined to extinction in the vast death of the solar sys-
> tem, and…the whole temple of Man's achievement
> must inevitably be buried beneath the debris of a

universe in ruins.... Only within the scaffolding of
these truths, only on the firm foundation of unyield-
ing despair, can the soul's habitation henceforth be
safely built.... Brief and powerless is Man's life; on
him and all his race the slow, sure doom falls pitiless
and dark. Blind to good and evil, reckless of destruction, omnipotent matter rolls its relentless way."[1]

Grim stuff. No wonder the atheist H. J. Blackham said the most drastic objection to atheism was its pointlessness: "It's too bad to be true." The good news is, not only do we not want to believe it, we don't have to.

If Christ is to be believed, when we come to "the end," there's God! When his dismayed followers sensed their cozy little world was about to end, the Master said, "Believe in God, believe also in me" (John 14:1, RSV). We are to *trust* God and think noble things of him. He's our assurance for the future.

The end isn't a comet on a collision course with earth or the vast silent death of a solar system, pitch-black, sunless, freezing, mo-tionless, and utterly lifeless. The end isn't a triumphant cancer or a mangled body and a drunk driver. The end isn't suicide and a lonely derelict; it isn't a strangled victim and a callous burglar. The end isn't a long ride in a black limousine and the clang of a cemetery gate.

In this life we'll have trouble and heartache, but that isn't the end. We'll see war and hear rumors of wars, but that isn't the end. There'll be earthquakes and floods, famines and hurricanes, but they aren't the end. When we come to the end, we'll find God! And whatever else the wilderness has or doesn't have, God is there.

In the meantime, we look at life's harsh realities with steady eyes, unlike King Xerxes who didn't allow bad news to enter his presence.[2] We look at the grinding circumstances of the world's millions—our own included—often tearfully, sometimes with groans and pleas, but always believing, however falteringly, that the last word isn't with circumstances; it's with God! And in God we trust!

Here are three major texts for people in trouble:

> For the past troubles will be forgotten
>> and hidden from my eyes.
> Behold, I will create
>> new heavens and a new earth.
> The former things will not be remembered,
>> nor will they come to mind.
> But be glad and rejoice forever
>> in what I will create,
> for I will create Jerusalem to be a delight
>> and its people a joy. (Isaiah 65:16-18)

> Since everything will be destroyed in this way, what kind of people ought you to be? You ought to live holy and godly lives as you look forward to the day of God and speed its coming. That day will bring about the destruction of the heavens by fire, and the elements will melt in the heat. But in keeping with his promise we are looking forward to a new heaven and a new earth, the home of righteousness. (2 Peter 3:11-13)

> Then I saw a new heaven and a new earth, for the first
> heaven and the first earth had passed away, and there
> was no longer any sea. (Revelation 21:1)

In each of these passages the prophets see the cursed world coming to an end in blood and fire and smoke, but when it vanishes they see a new heaven and a new earth, brimming with life, and God is the source of it. God's promise isn't empty—mourning *will* be turned to joy, life *will* conquer death, one day we *will* be done with the wilderness. A new world in which dwells righteousness *will* arrive, for God says he will bring it, and his promise is sure.

It's never been the way of God's people—even those under awful pressure—to believe that suffering and tragedy have the last word. Remember how Habakkuk "yielded his flickering torch" when God told him that "tanks" would be rumbling through the streets of his city, that there'd be derelict houses, deserted city squares, ethnic cleansing, mass graves, raped and butchered men, women, and children? Listen to the prophet's response:

> I hear, and I tremble within;
>> my lips quiver at the sound.
> Rottenness enters into my bones,
>> and my steps tremble beneath me.
> I wait quietly....
> Though the fig tree does not blossom,
>> and no fruit is on the vines;
> though the produce of the olive fails
>> and the fields yield no food;

though the flock is cut off from the fold,

and there is no herd in the stalls,

Yet I will rejoice in the LORD;

I will exult in the God of my salvation.

GOD, the Lord, is my strength;

he makes my feet like the feet of a deer,

and makes me tread upon the heights.

(3:16-19, NRSV)

The prophet knew that a redemptive purpose and a glorious assurance were behind God's outpoured wrath. God creates the wilderness on his way to creating a new world. He makes humanity homeless before giving us a glorious and permanent home. The prophet grasped and took refuge in this astonishing truth: The wilderness is doomed and a new world's coming!

When faced with the wilderness, those in Israel who were prone to heart failure, that is trust failure, said they would rather have died in bed in Egypt, eating and drinking. And that makes sense, for who wants a future of nothing but desert and hardship? And who wants a life of one marital brawl after another? Who wants a life that's nothing but one more hypodermic needle, one more battery of tests, one more night of pain, one more year of loneliness, one more year of moral wrestling and losing, one more year of self-loathing and fear, one more year in a job that crushes the soul and deadens the heart, one more year in a pigsty trying to make ends meet, one more decade of pointlessness? Who could want it? Why not end it all?

Because God has promised and he doesn't lie!

Year after long year enslaved Israelites worked until they were exhausted, seven days a week, their families and babies under threat of death. They must have dreamed of rebellion and freedom. They woke in the mornings to see their enemies. They worked all day in the presence of their enemies. They went home and watched their enemies spy on them. Everywhere they saw their enemies, day after week after month after year. Then one day Moses said, "Do not be afraid. Stand firm and you will see the deliverance the LORD will bring you today. The Egyptians you see today you will never see again" (Exodus 14:13).

The wilderness is not forever. It was never meant to be the destiny of God's creatures, and all who give themselves to him in trust will find deliverance: The enemy you see today, the one you've had to endure all your lifetime, you will never see him again! There's a day coming—because in the end there's God—when you'll walk down to the rim of some great sea and look at the enemies you've faced, enemies that were too strong for you, enemies who cut you, bled you until you cried out in shame. But they'll be dead, gone forever. Not because you became wiser or stronger or read some book or heard some special sermon, but because God stepped in, however he does these things, and put an end to them.

You'll understand then, even if like Job you receive no explanation. You'll understand that there was a reason for your long wilderness experience. In your unspeakable joy you'll be content to know that in the end there's God.

◀◀◀

The God
of the Wilderness

19

THE GOD WHO LOVES
WITHOUT LIMITS

He is the atoning sacrifice for our sins, and not only for ours
but also for the sins of the whole world.

1 JOHN 2:2

We're so unlike God. And to make matters worse, we have a distorted vision of who he is and what he's like. This difference between us and him is not simply that he has infinitely more power—it's a love issue. The difference is maybe seen best in the way he and we look at sinners (in our case, fellow sinners).

Let me say it again: God loves humanity! *Sinful* humanity! Hater and implacable enemy of sin though he is, he loves transgressors. He sees humanity as selfish, smug and self-righteous, downright wicked—and loves us still. He enjoys our company, has compassion on us in our need and blindness, defends us against the upright critics, and insists we're more valuable than a world of treasure and power. What else will explain his choosing to become part of that nation of sinners in the wilderness? On one occasion he said, "Sell yourself. Go ahead, sell yourself even for *a world,* and I tell you you've made a bad bargain."[1] This he says even of his enemies!

We, on the other hand, often love only what humanity *should* be. We rejoice only in the not-yet-existent person. We barely tolerate the one standing before us, and then our tolerance lasts only as long as it appears we can hope for change. We feel awkward and uncomfortable in the presence of sinners. We feel relief only if we can tell ourselves that we "set them straight" before we strode off. Our stingy obsession that someone out there is getting away with something is so unlike the joyful Lord who sought the company of sinners and so unlike the attracting, drawing, and *holy* Christ who was sought by the sinners and outcasts.

Christ said: "Here I am! I stand at the door and knock. If anyone hears my voice and opens the door, I will come in and eat with him, and he with me" (Revelation 3:20). The living Christ said this to a church no one would brag on; to a church that told him they didn't need him; to a church that was poor, naked, blind, pitiful, and wretched, though they thought they were the cream of the crop. Above all the other things they needed, they desperately needed a door-knocking Christ who, despite his revulsion against their sin, loved them and longed to have the profound intimacy of table fellowship with them.

All people—sinners and saints alike—matter to God!

And that's really it, isn't it? It's how much people matter to us and the pleasure we find in being with them that determines how far we'll go with them. Joyful love makes the difference. The elder brother in the story of the prodigal son had no joy or commitment to his prodigal brother. He was content to be "saved" without his brother, content to be right with his father by himself. He *missed* no one, felt no loss that the brother was lost. He was upright and law-abiding, and that became his snare. Absorbed in his own correctness, he became loveless, and in being loveless and contemptuous, he lost his father's likeness.

Haven't you wondered why it is that we make so many excuses for ourselves and so few for others? Yes, yes, I know that honor and holiness count! But doesn't God know that? Why, then, does he miss us so when we're gone in our unholy ways? Why can't he content himself with ninety-nine upright ones? Why does it bring him such joy when he finds the self-destructive one? Why is he for whom holiness and honor *really* count so anxious to save us from what we most assuredly deserve?

Love really does cover a multitude of sins. It doesn't deny their existence, doesn't say they're of no consequence, but it does defend the loved one because love refuses to believe that the loved one's flaws are the sum of his life. Their wrongs are wrong, of course, but we don't make the wrongs the index of their complete lives. Love sees in its own way. Why is it that though we know our spouses better than anyone else in the world, know their flaws—flaws unknown to anyone else—we brag on them so? If someone criticizes our mate, why do we have to suppress a growing anger or, at least, a rising irritation? Lovers will defend the loved one even to the point of taking or sharing the blame for the wrongs by saying things like, "If only I had…" Lovers never think of isolating a transgressing loved one, of leaving that person on his or her own. We only do that to people we care little about!

A man once gave me a prolonged and merciless verbal beating. As I was leaving, getting into my car, he said, in a sincere tone, "My door's always open."

I said, "You're kidding, aren't you?"

The poor man might even to this day say, "I offered to help him if he was in trouble!" But an offer of help is more than a phrase, even a sincerely spoken phrase. It's an atmosphere, an attitude, a tone. An offer of help is more than well-organized words. It's an invitation that's *lived out;* it's a sound that's made credible and real by a consistent behavior. It's a costly commitment, and it can't be thrown at the needy across a gulf created by "the righteous" who themselves are sinners. Even a dog will choose not to come to a savage owner, no matter how softly he says, "Come here…there's a good boy."

No, the God who came to live in Israel knew the people for who they were, yet he refused to despise them. He rescued them and came to live in them so that they could walk with their heads held high. He was the one who insisted that a man shouldn't be overly punished or "your brother will be degraded in your eyes" (Deuteronomy 25:3). Now there's a text that needs to be brought out into the light more often. God insists that the sinning brother mustn't be overly punished! But note the reason carefully. He mustn't be overly punished in case those punishing him see him as degraded. It's well known that unjust treatment can make a person feel degraded; what isn't so well known is that the person who does the punishing can come to see that person as worthless.

In the name of God, leave us the God who loves us all and longs to dwell with us. The God who will sit down and eat with us in intimate fellowship and fullness of joy. Leave us the God who can look sinful Israel in the eye and say slowly, compassionately, and with forethought, "I will…not despise you" (Leviticus 26:11, TLB).

Atheist Friedrich Wilhelm Nietzsche lost his faith in early life and came to despise people in general. He had respect for Jesus Christ, but he had only contempt for Christians, whom he said made sniveling wimps out of people. Too lazy to become strong, he said, they made strength a vice and cowardice a virtue. Humans, if we were to believe Nietzsche, were gutless, but with the "death of God," he assured us, a new kind of human was coming. A "superman" whose virtue would be that he would unashamedly pursue strength and denounce the weakening virtues of humility and compassion. This superman would be the *true* human and would gain what humanity in its heart longed for but didn't have the guts to pursue to the end: absolute power.

Though he was willing to pay the price for his creed, Nietzsche was wrong. Dead wrong. A philosophy like that generates misery. To think like that is to close the door to joy in what lies before us.

Ironically, those who have made a stone-hearted God in their own image have a theology similar to Nietzsche's philosophy. Because they focus on what humanity should be, they miss the glory of what humanity *is*. This creates terrific tensions within. Those who read their Bibles, obsessed with the sins and failures of others, can only gravitate to the darker passages. Stringing them together like beads on a string, they distort the grand drift of Scripture. Tirelessly rehearsing the truths about human sinfulness, they miss the grand optimism of the Bible, and they miss the pleasure God has in the humanity he has created.

Human sinfulness obliterates, for them, the wonder of humans; it obliterates the astonishing nature of a man or woman, a boy or girl. People who have made God in their image ooh and aah over a lovely landscape and turn up their noses at a human who doesn't share their theology. They rejoice at the mystique surrounding the mist-shrouded Golden Gate Bridge, but they feel little more than contempt when looking at a human who must struggle against sin.

They miss the fact that God really *does* love *sinners*. God doesn't love people because we're good; he loves people *because he made us*. But it isn't true that he loves us simply because we exist. We exist because he loves us.

The critics aren't able to sit and watch people and rejoice that God has given them life. The critics' *image* of what people should be gives them pleasure, but they can't rejoice that people actually exist, can't rejoice in the truth that they exist because God chooses that they exist. And despite the clear biblical message, the critics think Jesus agrees with them.

But they have missed the heart of Jesus by a million miles. While he was being put to death on the cross, Christ prayed, "Father, forgive them, for they do not know what they are doing" (Luke 23:34). God saw people exactly for what they were and are, and *then* he commended his love toward them in Jesus Christ. God didn't love them if they were as they should be, his love was—*is*—redemptive! Loving us as we are, he works to save us, and part of that saving process is making us, by his grace, what we can and will be.

God rejoices in his creation, fallen though it is. "Ah, the sinner's back!" he cries, calling his friends. "Let's have a party." Smug self-righteousness leads us to rewrite the parable to say that the father loves the prodigal only after he has returned. That isn't what the parable says at all! Prodigals are loved even when they're up to their eyes in piggery.

And when they're drawn home by memories of home, they're welcomed. Jesus welcomes sinners. *Welcomes* them! Can you see him welcome them with a grim look on his face? That can't be right; that would have been how Simon the Pharisee welcomed Christ into his home. No, if Christ ever smiled, if he ever made people feel at home, it was on those occasions when he both welcomed sinful humans and even ate with them. He hadn't lost his heart in his holiness.

Why did the blessed and only, one true God in the person of Jesus of Nazareth come into this wilderness? Why did he go to the cross? "For God so loved the world that He gave His only begotten Son" (John 3:16, NKJV).

This is the one true God and Father of our Lord Jesus Christ! What else explains his long, long patience as he journeys with us through this wilderness of a world to bring us home?

20

THE GOD WHO GLIMPSES GLORY IN FOOLS

No! But this mob that knows nothing of the law—
there is a curse on them.

JOHN 7:49

When he saw the crowds, he had compassion on them, because
they were harassed and helpless, like sheep without a shepherd.

MATTHEW 9:36

When Balak wanted Israel cursed, he thought he had good reason for it. Like the land-hungry multitude at the time of the great Oklahoma Land Rush, they were poised on the edge of the desert ready to invade his land and take it from him. He was wrong about them, of course, but that's what he thought, so he sent for the prophet Balaam and asked him to curse Israel.

The prophet really wanted to curse Israel and line his pockets, but in the end, unwilling though he was, he spoke God's blessing on the pilgrim nation. We're told that Balaam got up on one of the summits of Mount Peor and:

turned his face toward the desert. When Balaam looked out and saw Israel encamped tribe by tribe, the Spirit of God came upon him and he uttered his oracle:

"The oracle of Balaam son of Beor...
the oracle of one who hears the words of God,
    who sees a vision from the Almighty,
    who falls prostrate, and whose eyes are opened:

"How beautiful are your tents, O Jacob,
    your dwelling places, O Israel!" (Numbers 24:1-5)

When you think that this nation was sitting down there only because Moses had pleaded with God not to obliterate it, when you remember that these were the people who broke God's heart and his laws with their golden calf, when you remember that God foretold their future wickedness even after he gave them the land—when you think of all this, it comes as a surprise to hear God look down on Israel and say, "How beautiful are your tents, O Jacob." What is this? Is God the Divine Dupe who can't see or fathom Israel's character? Or does God see *in a way* we can't see? Maybe the problem doesn't lie with God at all, but with us.

If Balak rather than God had spoken of the Israelites, we'd have a very different description of them, precisely because Balak cared nothing about them. Your heart determines what you see, don't you think? Isn't the proof of that everywhere?

Take Miguel de Cervantes' *Don Quixote,* which is arguably the best novel ever written. Cervantes says it's a parody on the romantic notions of chivalry, which means that's what he started out to write. Is that what he finally delivered—a sarcastic look at sentimentality and silliness? No. It's a damning indictment of our sinful blindness!

Having laid down the melancholy burden of sanity, Don Quixote becomes a knight. But before he's carried back home in a cage, he shows himself courteous, gentle, brave, and long-suffering. Unless there's some evil enchantment, all the women he meets are beautiful and worthy of the greatest respect, and the men (most of them) are assumed to be good and noble. In return for all this, he's beaten, mocked, and humiliated.

Literary giant, J. B. Priestley, gives us this piercing insight:

> On one level it is merely laughable that Don Quixote should mistake a miserable inn for a castle, the landlord for a generous custodian, the village whores for ladies of quality, a mean supper for a noble feast. On the level below, all this seems tragic; it is the butt of the company, the man out of his wits, who sees what everybody ought to be seeing, if our values were really what we claim them to be, if Christendom existed outside our sermons and dreams....
>
> [H]ow does the world behave when it is challenged by Don Quixote and his illusions? It laughs but its complacency is shattered, there is anger in its laughter, and so it daubs his long mild face with mud, thumps and cudgels his bony frame, and tries to beat the nonsense about knight, high chivalry, spells and enchantment, out of him. But this angry brutal world

> itself is under a wicked spell, has become its own spite-
> ful enchanter.... And below this could be tragic irony
> again, that what is better is derided and defeated
> by the worse, that a madness overcomes a glorious
> madness.[1]

Your heart determines how you see and what you see.

In the *Expository Times,* editor C. S. Rodd rehearses an incident told by Russell Maltby that's both painful and glorious. Maltby was acquainted with a man whose wife left him for another shortly after their marriage. She came back and the husband welcomed her home. But this happened again and again, her going to the other man and her husband giving her his heart and a home on her return.

A friend of the abused husband spoke to him, wanting to commiserate with and comfort him, but the husband stopped him with a terse, "Not a word! She's my wife." She returned home after a final absence, and some time later died in her patient and loving husband's arms.

Rodd shared this story with an assembly one morning, and a marriage counselor, on his way out of the building, remarked to Rodd that the husband's "psychological problems needed to be looked at."[2]

Maybe, maybe not. If the husband had been firmer, would his wife have responded differently? Should he have given her an ultimatum? Who can say? But it's interesting to me that this marriage counselor, who knew nothing more about the situation than you and I do, was perfectly willing to see the husband as a disturbed man. The man who was gladly paying an awful price in this painful situation is seen as needing therapy?

So often we see what we're looking for. We shouldn't have to be told this, but we forget it so easily. We look at someone we adore and the physical blemishes don't exist—what others call blemishes are interesting variations. We look at our enemy whose failings are no greater than our own or those we love, and what do we do? We see nothing but his failures. Am I wrong in thinking that's how it usually is with us?

When we approach Scripture, the situation's the same. Some of us are fooled into thinking we come without presuppositions, without preferences, without prejudices. This isn't humanly possible and is made doubly impossible because sin *does* affect how we judge matters. If our love pool is shallow, then we soon ferret out and give extra weight to the texts that say people should bear their own burdens. If we're strong on doctrinal correctness, then we gravitate to those texts that speak of nonnegotiable truths and work back from there to a position where almost every question is a jugular issue on which life hangs. If we're blessed by strength of character but lack patience, we expound passages on growth and sanctification while merely quoting texts on God's long-suffering.

I don't wish to oversimplify, but isn't it interesting that God presents himself as the patient husband of an unfaithful wife all over the Bible and especially in the book of Hosea?[3] I don't say we know all God knows or that we can follow him in all his ways, but I am saying that maybe we lack his heart.

Your heart determines what you see because it determines how you see! God looks at wayward Israel and calls her beautiful. The prodigal's father sees his returned son as a source of joy; the brother saw him as a heathen rewarded for his wicked absence.

If we're cynical and look out our window, we see a host of devious, self-serving louts. If you're Harry O'Connor you see...? If you're Jill Smith you see...? And if you're God you see...?

God created us, and even though we turned against him, he came looking for us to bring us home. The upright saw the people as a mob (John 7:49), but Christ saw them as "sheep without a shepherd" (Matthew 9:36), harassed and helpless. This way of seeing things and people is characteristic of God. He looks at Simon and sees Peter, but he loves Simon even before he is Peter. God doesn't simply love what a man or woman can become by his grace; he loves them because that's how he is.

Down below our squalor and filth, down below our smugness and self-righteousness, down below our studied indifference to what's right or wrong, down below all the sin and shame we've covered ourselves with, God sees something he loves. And if he loves it, there's got to be something glorious about it.

Again, it's not that God doesn't see our sin. He sees it more clearly than we can know he sees it. His rage against it knows no bounds, and we, in our moments when we're most like him and passionately hate that foul thing, merely play at hating it. He who hates sin with a perfect and consummate hatred has still looked on us and loved us. He who has looked on us and pitied us still comes running to our side when we shame ourselves and hurt him and others.

All this is true! How else can we explain 1 John 2:1, where John says he's writing so that we don't sin. "But if anybody does sin," he adds, "we have one who speaks to the Father in our defense."

Why would the spotless and holy Christ run to defend us before

God when we've sinned? How could he defend sin? He couldn't and he doesn't. It isn't sin he defends—it's us! Christ speaks in our defense. Wouldn't you like to hear what he says? Wouldn't you like to hear what he says to a Father who so loves you that he gave his Son as an atoning sacrifice for the whole world (1 John 2:2)? What would he say? How would he phrase it? What would his first words be?

"Ah, Father, he's struggling the best he can. Sin has made an awful mess of him, but you and I have set his heart alight and shown him his darkness, and he's learning to hate it. We've given him a vision of freedom, and he likes it and wants more. We've given him a sense of purpose, and it's made a huge difference in how he sees life. But he and the world, he and his family, he and his friends, he and his society have developed deep, sinful patterns in him so it isn't easy for him to be done with it."

Maybe he'd say that. And he'd also speak of the love the Father has for us. "How great is the love the Father has lavished on us" (1 John 3:1). Somewhere in his defense the Master would "plead the blood" on behalf of his sinning sister or brother, for that in the end is our only defense.

"Father, we knew they'd shame themselves and sin against us. This comes as no surprise to us and the love we have for them—for all of them, without exception—we've expressed in our atoning sacrifice and it's that that I come reminding you of. Your child is in trouble again and needs our forgiveness and cleansing. He comes confessing all this."

And in this profoundly merciful and pitying Jesus Christ, God sees the flawless image of himself—and sees glory. In this faithful, patient, interceding Christ, the Father sees himself and sees a sovereignty and majesty that are seen best as they express themselves in glorious kindness and everlasting good will toward those he has made.

And

I

really

can't   grasp

a bit

of

what

I've

just

written.

21

THE GOD WHO
IS GENEROUS

But because of his great love for us,
God, who is rich in mercy, made us alive with Christ
even when we were dead in transgressions.

EPHESIANS 2:4-5

The God of the wilderness is generous and shows his mercy to a thousand generations. In the wilderness the Israelites wanted for nothing. The prophet Isaiah speaks of a God who offers abundant pardon. Paul and Peter speak of his richness in mercy. John speaks of the magnitude of love God lavishes on us. How reassuring that he's like this; assuring us all since we all have to call on that generosity without ceasing.

But many of us who speak most about his generosity are prone to deny it to others.[1] At least this was so for the Italian composer Antonio Salieri. Salieri officially served Emperor Joseph II for thirty-six years at the court in Vienna as master of the chapel, though he'd been around the court for much longer. He was a great composer who produced thirty-nine operas, seven secular cantatas, and eighty-two religious compositions, plus an assortment of other pieces. He remained friendly with Franz Joseph Haydn and Ludwig van Beethoven throughout his life and had given Beethoven lessons in counterpoint. Beethoven dedicated the three violin sonatas, Opus 12, to Salieri.

When he was a teenager, Salieri dedicated himself to God. As the movie *Amadeus* (which took *many* liberties with history) tells the story, one day he prayed, "Lord, make me a great composer. Let me celebrate your glory through music. Make me famous dear God; make me immortal. After I die, let people forever speak my name with love for what I wrote. In return, I will give you my chastity, my industry, my deepest humility, every hour of my life." Salieri thoroughly believed God gave him his giftedness.

Salieri became the toast of Europe, and on June 16, 1816, he celebrated the golden anniversary of his debut in Vienna. Everyone who mattered was there, and some of his famous pupils, including Franz Schubert, played pieces in his honor. Life couldn't have been better for him. He received invitations from everywhere, everyone praised him and sought his opinion without fail; he was part of every tribunal, but something troubled him deeply, and his life soured and shriveled.

Let's turn the clock back to more than twenty-five hundred years before Salieri, to another musician and composer by the name of Asaph. When David brought the ark to Jerusalem, Asaph was one of the lead singers. He was apparently the "master of the chapel" for the most revered king in Israelite history.[2]

Today, three thousand years after he wrote them, the songs Asaph composed are still being sung and read in the presence of millions. Twelve psalms bear his name to the glory of God.[3]

What did Salieri and Asaph have in common? Both were troubled by God's generosity, though they didn't realize it. Both were troubled, not by bad things happening to good people so much as by good things happening to bad people.

In Psalm 73 Asaph says he almost lost his footing when he saw what was happening in the lives of those who were bad. They prospered and people sang their praises while he and other good people like him were ignored and had to worry about making ends meet. He wanted to know how this could be so.

The success of Wolfgang Amadeus Mozart drove Salieri to distraction. Mozart is regarded as "the most sheerly musical composer who ever lived" and was seen by Johann Wolfgang von Goethe as "the human incarnation of a divine force of creation."[4] Mozart began composing at four years of age, and he continued furiously, with hardly a breath, until he died at age thirty-five.

It isn't surprising that Salieri would be jealous, even though the Viennese public preferred his best-known Italian (through the French) work *Axur, re d'Ormus*. On the whole, people were thrilled and pleased by his music, but they were dumbfounded by Mozart, whose name was never off their lips and whose music left them speechless with pleasure. Not only did Mozart write more than Salieri, his scores were perfectly written the first time—he didn't revise!

In the movie *Amadeus,* Salieri described Mozart as "a boastful, lustful, smutty, infantile boy!" Every time he heard Mozart's name—worse, every time he heard him praised—he became more incensed. Finally, obsessed by his jealousy and after looking at some of Mozart's perfectly written scores, he throws a crucifix into the fire, saying to God, "We are enemies you and I, because you are unjust, unfair, unkind. I will hinder and harm your creature on earth as far as I am able." Unjust and unkind? Because he poured his rich, creative blessing down on a child? God is unjust because he is generous?

Darkness closed in on Salieri; he shriveled and died many years before they put his body in the ground. In spite of still making the rounds, showing up at the various places, being recognized in a crowd and praised, he was a shell, withered on the inside.

If we ourselves didn't struggle with envy and jealousy, if we weren't disturbed by questions about good things and bad people, if we weren't inclined to stand in for God as the righteous judge, perhaps all this would be of historical interest to us but not relevant. But at times we, too, see ourselves as wise enough to do God's job for him. At times we stand utterly offended that God is generous, even to those who care nothing for him. At times we think Jonah had an unanswerable case against God, and Nineveh should have gone down in blood and fire and smoke. At times we rot because of envy and wither through jealousy.

As it was with Salieri, so it is with us, for when we burn with that kind of fever, everyone loses. The one we're in a fever about loses any help we might give him and gets only our ill will. We can't speak or act in appreciation of him, can't help him to rise to better heights, can't influence him for the good. We only know how to punish him (which is what we mean when we say we want to hold him responsible). Not being generous ourselves, we find it too difficult even to be fair!

And we lose! The goodness or usefulness of our enemy's life and work is lost on us. Others are lifted nearer to God and a lovelier life because they are able to appreciate whatever good God is doing through our enemy. Not us! We're too consumed with our correct view of his shortcomings, too filled with bile because we know he is sinfully fragile, too busy dissecting him to be helped by whatever wisdom, grace, or goodness he brings with him.

Even God loses, as in the example of Eleanor. God is doing marvelous things through her. She speaks to God's glory and people are transformed. She's compassionate and honest, caring and generous, patient and brave—but she's flawed. She struggles in the direction of the light of God, but those who know her best know she has lost some major battles in the past and stumbles even yet. She will not give up the battle because she can't, and all the while she echoes around the music of Christ.

So angry are we at Eleanor because of her blunders that we become her enemy and won't allow God to get the glory he exhibits in her. Rather than have people lifted up to God by her "success" for God, we would destroy Eleanor. If God is depending on her to bring him glory, as far as we're concerned, he can do without it! In short, Salieri and we would rob God of glory just so we can keep it from the Mozarts of the world.

There's something arrogant about calling God's justice into question or appointing oneself the cursing executioner when God himself has chosen to bless the one we choose to curse. If only we would allow God to do the judging!

> The decision is announced by messengers, the holy
> ones declare the verdict, so that the living may know
> that the Most High is sovereign over the kingdoms of

men and gives them to anyone he wishes and sets over them the lowliest of men. (Daniel 4:17)

A man can receive only what is given him from heaven. (John 3:27-28)

The apostles also struggled with God's justice. They are shocked when Christ tells the rich young ruler that he has to sell all he has in order to enter the kingdom of heaven. They asked Jesus, "Who then can be saved?" (Matthew 19:25). Peter and the others are afraid that they, who've sacrificed so much, will be left empty-handed. Certain that their sacrifice put them in the front line, they wanted to know what they were going to gain.

That's when the Master told the story of the different groups of workers hired at various times on the same day to work in a man's vineyard.

> When evening came, the owner of the vineyard said to his foreman, "Call the workers and pay them their wages, beginning with the last ones hired and going on to the first."
>
> The workers who were hired about the eleventh hour came and each received a denarius. So when those came who were hired first, they expected to receive more. But each one of them also received a denarius. When they received it, they began to grumble against the landowner. "These men who

were hired last worked only one hour," they said, "and you have made them equal to us who have borne the burden of the work and the heat of the day."

But he answered one of them, "Friend, I am not being unfair to you. Didn't you agree to work for a denarius? Take your pay and go. I want to give the man who was hired last the same as I gave you. Don't I have the right to do what I want with my own money? Or are you envious because I am generous?" (Matthew 20:8-15)

In the end, those who worked longest thought they should have been paid more than the others. Well, that's not quite the truth. More precisely, they thought the others should not have been paid as much. They knew they had been paid what was agreed and were angry that the master of the house had given the latecomers a generous wage. When the jealous ones complained, the master of the house said, "Don't I have the right to do what I want with my own money? Or are you envious because I am generous?"

What a Lord! There must be a jillion ways in which God differs from us, but God help us, in this area it must be especially marked. I'm generalizing, of course, but we're so stingy and Scrooge-like. And what makes it worse, we can spot a Scrooge a mile off and despise him for it.

I don't need to rehearse Charles Dickens's *A Christmas Carol* to remind you how miserly Ebenezer Scrooge was. (What a name for Scrooge—*Ebenezer,* which means "God has helped me get this far"). For him, all talk of Christmas with its notions of giving and kindness and generosity were met with, "Bah! Humbug!" until he was changed. And when he was changed, he didn't merely become fair, he became generous. He lavished money everywhere, on boys who ran errands for him, on employees and orphanages. He lavished praise and smiles on everything from turkeys to babies, and he made the community around him a new and wonderful place to live.

How unlike God he had been. How like God he became.

I don't remember who said it, but it's true, "We're never more like God than when we give."

A story from immediately after World War II strikes the same note. A young boy stood looking into a bakery shop window, drooling at all that was on display. All he had was an empty stomach and pockets to match. An American serviceman watched for a moment, stepped inside the shop, got the boy's attention, and asked him to point out the things he thought were best. One after another the shopkeeper put the items in a bag while the child laughed at the game they were playing through the window. Finally done, the soldier came out and put the big bag of goodies into the arms of the wide-eyed child and walked off with a smile. He turned when he heard the astonished boy shout after him, "Hey, mister, are you God?"

The God of the wilderness is lavish in his love and generosity, and, oh, how we need his generosity to cover our wrongdoing. And who can say, perhaps God's kindness to our enemy is to bring him to repentance. Should we deny the sinner repentance as well as praise?

It's the glory of God that he cares at all about any of us. It's the glory of God that leads him to give us any of his gifts, and much more that he longs to dwell with and in us. It's the glory of God that he loves the whole world so much that he gave us his Son to bring life to us. It's the glory of God that he allowed the nations to walk away from him into their wicked ways, yet he gave them fruitful seasons and filled their hearts with joy (Acts 14:17). And those whom God in his generosity has honored are not to be despised by anyone!

Instead of being plagued with envy when God blesses others, maybe our response will be profound gratitude that we are ourselves are able to say:

> Whom have I in heaven but you?
>> And earth has nothing I desire besides you.
> My flesh and my heart may fail,
>> but God is the strength of my heart
>> and my portion forever. (Psalm 73:25-26)

22

THE GOD WHO ASKS FOR ENTRANCE

When Israel was a child, I loved him....
But the more I called Israel, the further they went
from me.... My people are determined to turn from me....
How can I give you up, Ephraim?

HOSEA 11:1-2,7-8

Danish philosopher Sören Kierkegaard was furious with those philosophers who theorized and harmonized all reality, God included, into reason and logic. He insisted that these philosophers, particularly G. W. F. Hegel, murdered life. He was angry, too, with the Danish church for doing the same thing from another angle: While Hegel executed life, the church bled it white. As Kierkegaard saw it, the church preached a Christianity that made no demands, had no commitment, believed that "anything goes." As a result, people had a pathetic image of God and were dying of boredom. God was no longer the God of Abraham who demanded outrageous things and complete obedience; he was a poor, pitiable figure who stood cap in hand at our doors while we decided if we wanted to let him in. The Dane has a lot to say—a lot we need to hear—about the easy-going, anxious-to-please, almost groveling God we hear so much about today in evangelical and other circles.

The gospel is more than an invitation. When Paul preached the good news that Jesus was king, it was more than an invitation to "let Jesus into your heart"; it was an affirmation that Christ was king, whether we liked it or not. Still, Paul Scherer is right. If all the dusty miles from Bethlehem to Golgotha prove anything, they prove that places exist where raw power can't enter, and the human heart is one of them. In Christ, God comes announcing himself as sovereign, but a sovereign offering friendship and life to rebels.

We see this when the God who created galaxies and rolled out space like a man rolling out a carpet comes to Moses and says: "Tell the Israelites to bring me an offering. You are to receive the offering for me from each man *whose heart prompts him to give....* Then have them make a sanctuary for me, and I will dwell among them" (Exodus 25:2,8, emphasis added). God wants the Israelites to build a tabernacle so that he can live with them. The initiative, of course, is God's, and he doesn't stand back and merely watch Israel build the tabernacle. The Spirit of God gives the skill and heart to the workers, but he also stresses the free-will nature of the offering and the work of building the tabernacle.

Read Exodus 35 for yourself. It's hardly God coming with hat in hand, but it is God treating the Israelites like humans rather than mindless chess pieces. He has been willing to give humans the possibility of a creative response to his gift, which is life with him. Exactly how God's sovereignty and humanity's choosing mesh is beyond me, but Scripture clearly states that God is sovereign and that we're allowed to say yes or no to him. I'm not suggesting that our yes or no is given without factors that help shape them—of course not. I am saying that whatever factors come together to make up my yes, it is *my* yes and not someone else's.

God must be wanted, he must be loved. He prefers an honest Job with all his blind anger to the heartless obedience of religious yes-men.[1]

"Here I am! I stand at the door and knock. If anyone hears my voice and opens the door, I will come in and eat with him, and he with me" (Revelation 3:20). The ruler of God's creation and Lord of the churches[2] knocks on that door. He knows precisely who he is and announces himself as such. Still, he presents himself as a door knocker and not as someone who smashes in the gate of the heart.

William Barclay's commentary on this passage tells us that the Greek word for "eat" refers to the main, evening meal, not a meager breakfast or quick lunch. At the evening meal people would spend time with each other, communing and in no hurry to part. So what Christ offers is no quick "in and out" with the managing director. He's offering the warmth and joy of the best meal of the day. It's a two-way experience: We will eat with Christ and he will eat with us. He credits us with something to offer to his own personal joy.

Other gods, if we believe the stories, are willing to bully their creatures to get their way; not this one. God makes covenants with humans. In Hebrew 11 he praises certain individuals for making costly choices to his glory and urges others to follow their example. God seems to take seriously human obedience and human gallantry. For all his own involvement in producing it, God lays it at the feet of these lovely humans.

He sees what *they* have done—he sees their faith—and he exults in it. He sees their spirit and conduct, and we're told he was "not ashamed to be called their God."[3] In his paraphrase of this verse, Eugene Peterson turns this into a positive, "You can see why God is so proud of them" (MSG). All this implies that there's something for us to give to God, and while it's the result of the grace of God working in us, it's still grace that works in us and not an overwhelming assertion of God's omnipotent will. We aren't coerced![4]

How pleased God is when we adore him and volunteer our hearts as a home for him! How thrilled he is when his people welcome him into their midst as Lord and friend. We can guess his pleasure by looking at his heartbreak when they don't want him. "O Jerusalem, Jerusalem.... How often I wanted to gather your children together, as a hen gathers her chicks under her wings, but you were not willing!" (Matthew 23:37, NKJV). And he weeps over their rejection of him and their self-destruction.

When Christ rebukes the hard of heart for their willful blindness, he assures them it isn't for want of evidence and instruction that they reject him. It isn't that they haven't been invited; it's that they *won't* come. "You diligently study the Scriptures," he says, "because you think that by them you possess eternal life. These are the Scriptures that testify about me, yet you refuse to come to me to have life" (John 5:39-40). It's clear his audience hasn't been excluded by some eternal decree. God's offer to them to come and have life is genuine. It's also clear that their sinful hearts have led them to refuse that life.

A poet unknown to me said:

> *God loves to be longed for,*
> *He longs to be sought;*

For he sought us himself
With such longing and love.
He died for desire of us,
Marvelous thought;
And he longs for us now
To be with him above.

When humanity rebelled and walked away from him, God missed us and began the pursuit to woo us back. Of rebellious Israel he said, "But I will court her again and bring her into the wilderness, and I will speak to her tenderly there. There I will give back her vineyards to her and transform her Valley of Troubles into a Door of Hope" (Hosea 2:14-15, TLB). God doesn't force us into life with him; he pleads, calls, holds out his hands all day, courts us, or "speaks coaxingly"[5] to us. Should we be afraid of this kind of truth? Certainly not!

In Joshua 7 we see God's strange way of speaking coaxingly to Israel when they were in the Valley of Achor. The Valley of Achor was a place of national panic in Joshua's day. Achan and his family were stoned in the Valley of Achor because he had disobeyed God by stealing some of the plunder from the battle of Jericho. As a result of this disobedience, the Israelites lost the battle at Ai and thirty-six Israelites were killed. God used this fearful experience to bind Israel more closely to him. Listen, we're not to see God's severity as coercion; we're to see it as part of his pleading with us to return.

God wants us to want him! Does this cheapen him? He doesn't think so. God is infinite in power and majesty. He will not dishonor himself and is altogether pleased with who he is and will not accept a rival. While all this is true, we're not to think he has an identity crisis when humans don't return his love or if they rebel. He doesn't. He voluntarily laid aside divine privileges and came as Jesus Christ to win us back. He wears his almightiness well, and while creation expresses his power and glory, he doesn't strut about it as though it were the grand proof of his Godhood.

C. S. Lewis had it right:

> To be sovereign of the universe is no great matter to God. In Himself, at home in "the land of the Trinity," he is Sovereign of a far greater realm. We must keep always before our eyes that vision of Lady Julian's in which God carried in His hand, a little object like a nut, and that nut was "all that is made." God who needs nothing, loved into existence wholly superfluous creatures in order that He may love and perfect them.[6]

God loved us into existence in order to love us to perfection, and our faithful response to him triggers his joy. Incredible! How often have we been told that we can make God angry? How often have we been reminded that we can grieve God? Often! It's only fitting to say that we can also make God happy. "I tell you, there is rejoicing in the presence of the angels of God over one sinner who repents" (Luke 15:10). God sings with joy over his repentant and restored people.[7] Isn't that amazing?

To give God the glory due him, we mustn't make him all sovereign power. We must allow him to want to be wanted. Humans aren't their own saviors, and we must get around to confessing that without reservation. Nevertheless, God did give us free will. Our human experience is not God himself saying yes to his own invitation. It is our glad, thankful, and noncoerced yes to someone who has won our hearts and our allegiance by his wisdom and majesty and merciful request for entrance.

. The only true and living God asks the planet to invite him into its life. In doing this he isn't asking us to invest him with sovereignty; he's asking us to submit to it. That God laid down his life is a strange way of exercising sovereignty, but astonishing power is in that sacrifice. It is power perfected in weakness. It is omnipotent weakness.

Arthur Gossip, a chaplain in World War I, speaking about the power of the cross and how it works, offers us this:

> Well, once, far up the duckboard track towards Pachendaele—which those of you who were out yonder will agree was, by far, the most eerie and awesome part of the whole front in the last war—I came upon a laddie lying all alone and—dead. I don't know why, out of the multitude that one saw killed, he so impressed me. But he had given his life for us, given it in the spring and its first freshness. And I remember how—all alone in that grim lonesome wilderness of endless shell holes, mile upon mile of them, like a grey tumbling sea—I pulled off my bonnet, and looking down into his dead eyes, promised him that, because he had done this for us, I would see to it that his sacrifice was not in vain. "I promise you," said I, "that I will be a better man, because you have done this. I promise it."

And he goes on to say,

> All which was twenty-five years ago. And, in the main,
> I have largely forgotten. Yet, even now, at times, it rises
> up with the old vividness, and stings and shames me
> toward worthier things.[8]

This is how the cross of Christ works. This is how God asks an entrance.

23

THE GOD WHO
CONFRONTS OUR SIN

If thou, O LORD, shouldst mark iniquities,
Lord, who could stand? But there is forgiveness with thee,
that thou mayest be feared.

PSALM 130:3-4 (RSV)

God's sweet graciousness and unutterable longing to dwell with
humans in holy love is seen in the very existence of the tabernacle.
Without his hunger for our fellowship, there would have been no tabernacle, nor would God have sent his Son into the world. The tabernacle declared, "God has come to be with you, come on in!"

But the God who dwelt in the tabernacle was hidden behind
boards and curtains, hidden on the other side of sacrificial altars and
cleansing pools, hidden within a very sacred enclosure called the Holy
of Holies and wrapped in clouds of incense. All these obstacles made
one thing clear: Sinful humans can't *stroll* into God's presence or see it
as their inherent right. If it's a freedom, it's a holy freedom. If it's a
privilege, it's a gracious privilege. The obstacles reminded the wor-
shipers that their communion with God was a gift—a spellbinding,

almost-too-good-to-be-true gift. The high priest could enter the Holy of Holies only one day a year, and even then he had to bring with him the blood of an innocent sacrifice. The high priest came with bells on his garment, signaling that he was daring to approach this holy place, which swirled with clouds of incense that hid the glory of God and saved the priest, who would have died had he seen that glory.

God takes our sin more seriously than we ever could. That's because he understands it better than we, because he's holier than we, because he loves more than we. God doesn't hold us responsible for not hating sin as much as he does, because we can't—we're not God. Only God can hate sin as much as God does. It's true, of course, that the more we become like him, the more we'll despise our sins and love righteousness and purity.

Yet God doesn't forget our limitations. The psalmist's confession puts us in our place:

> As far as the east is from the west,
>> so far has he removed our transgressions from us.
> As a father has compassion on his children,
>> so the LORD has compassion on those who fear
>> him;
> for he knows how we are formed,
>> he remembers that we are dust. (103:12-14)

For…he remembers that we are dust. God knows how we've been shaped and how pathetic we are, and he makes allowances for that in how he works with us.

Job wants God to bear this in mind when he protests that God's keeping too strict an eye on him. He complains:

> Am I the sea, am I the Dragon, to be watched narrowly by thee?… What is man that thou dost make so much of him, fixing thy mind on him?… If I sin, what harm is that to thee, O thou Spy upon mankind? Why must thou always find me in thy way, why vex thyself with me? Why not forgive my guilt, why not let my sin pass? (7:12-21, MOFFATT)

"What do you expect of me?" Job wants to know. "I'm just another puny human, why come after me as though I were something more?"

So what has all this to do with God's confronting us with our sin? God is angry with us because we don't give him what we humans by his grace can and should give. Scripture rages about our greed, our unfaithfulness to our spouses, our abuse of our children, our denial of justice to our neighbors, our uncleanness, our ingratitude for life's blessings, our hoarding while others starve, our whining over inconveniences when others can barely stay alive. The sins God is angry about are the homegrown, very human variety. He doesn't say, "You are gods and you don't give me a god's obedience." He says we don't even give him a human's obedience! When the peevish Israelites wanted to know, "What does he want from us? Ten thousand rivers of oil? Child sacrifice?" the prophet said, "He has made it clear to you what he wants—a life characterized by humility, mercy and justice."[1]

Mere humans like ourselves can't commit superhuman sins; we're not majestic enough. Nevertheless, God expects from humans what humans, with his help, can give him. We aren't gods or titans, so he holds us responsible for human-size sins. For all the convolutions and mutations of our sins, they boil down to our refusal to give to God glad-hearted obedience, our refusal to love God and our neighbor as ourselves.

Even within human parameters we've got to maintain some modesty when confessing our sins. As the old doggerel verse reminds us, even when it comes to sinning we're not that great:

> *Once in a saintly passion*
> *I cried in deepest grief,*
> *"O God, my heart is filled with guile,*
> *Of sinners I'm the chief."*
> *Then stood my guardian angel*
> *And whispered from behind,*
> *"Vanity my little man,*
> *you're nothing of the kind."*

It isn't enough that we sin. God help us, we feel compelled to turn ourselves into tragic figures (which is another facet of our sin) who are *fated* to damnation—or at least we talk as though we felt that way. We seem to think that God's unfathomable, holy recoil to sin says something about the nature of our sin rather than something about his holiness. *It isn't about us!* We're not supposed to think things like, "My sin must be colossal, look at how God reacts to it." It'd be more in line to say, "God must be infinitely holy, look at how he recoils at mere human sin." Let me say it again: *It isn't about our sin, it's about his holiness!* But God isn't that easily put off; he loves us too much to settle for that.

He's probing and insistent and demanding. He won't allow us to wallow in our weakness, won't let us whine in gutless resignation. When we're tired of the struggle against evil, when we want to drift with the sinful currents, we'll talk about quitting and whine in a pseudo-nobility about our not being worthy of him. Of course we're not worthy of him, but he won't let us off that easily, won't let us walk away with a lie on our lips: "He couldn't want me. Not me." He *does* want us, and if we want nothing to do with *him*, then let's plainly say so rather than pretend we're more demanding than he is. "Yes, he'd let me in, he'd forgive me freely; it's just that I can't forgive myself!"

What pride and nonsense this is! As if forgiveness lay with us and not with God. The holy sovereign willingly forgives, but we, with our fathomless depths of holiness, are more offended by our sin than he is? More repulsed by our wickedness than he is? We can't forgive ourselves?

Better to confess openly: "I don't want to be forgiven. I don't want to hear that he loves and wants me still. I want to be free of him, want to feel no ties. It's easier to walk away from someone I think no longer wants me, so don't keep reminding me of his boundless love and infinite patience. Let me alone to enjoy my drifting, the delicious giving in to whatever suits my mood."

In confronting us with our sin, God does more than speak to us as individuals; he speaks to us a single humanity. As humans we're all bound up in one grand rebellion, feeding each other's sinful ways, strengthening one another in sinful attitudes and prejudices, nurturing in each other all that fragments us, even while we band together in a single, united rejection of God.

We'd like to distance ourselves from the unspeakable crimes some individuals and groups and nations have wallowed in. This gives us the grounds for self-righteousness. But God won't hold with this: *There is none righteous, no not one!* There may be many faces of humanity, but there's only one humanity. Looking at it from God's angle, it's not that some individual did this or that. It's that humanity, as seen in that individual, did this or that. Bitterness exists in the world, not because one man or woman is bitter, but because we've fed one another bitterness, because bitterness and racism and cruelty and greed express the character of a whole planet in rebellion.

God will not allow us to distance ourselves from the crimes of our fellow humans. For good or ill, we're united in one human family, and we make our contribution to the treason against God and the self-destruction of humanity. We'd like to go to God and say, "Here's my list of things done wrong and good things not done. I'd like you to judge me as an independent, free-standing human unit!"

We think that would cover it, but it won't. To some degree we are all implicated in each others' sin. The finger is not the foot, but it's no more and no less part of one body.

Yes, Scripture teaches individual responsibility for sin. We didn't rape the widow—one man did. We didn't abuse the child—one mother did. We didn't drop the bombs; we didn't embezzle the money; we didn't burn the building down with the people in it; we didn't douse the girl with kerosene and set fire to her. It's right to note that. Certainly specific individuals must be dealt with for doing these things; they are guilty, peculiarly guilty. They're guilty, but they're not *exclusively* guilty, for we have corrupted not only ourselves as individuals—we've helped to corrupt society and our fellow sinners in society. And others helped to corrupt us. We have all corrupted one another. "If a man is allured by the things of this world and is estranged from his Creator, it is not he alone who is corrupted, but the whole world is corrupted with him."[2]

How else do we explain the prophet Ezra's blushing face and his abject apology for sins of which he wasn't guilty? How else do we explain Daniel, trembling and clothed in sackcloth, begging for forgiveness for sin when he is one of the outstanding righteous people in the nation?[3]

While it's true that God is due and worthy of our sinless devotion, we can't give that, not in this phase of human history. We don't avoid all the evil or do all the good we can. Our hearts are injured, so our sin issues from "mission control."[4]

Sinlessness is beyond us, and the thundering denunciations we hear from God are not that we don't give him "sinlessness." Our crime is that we haven't even given him an affectionate respect and obedience, coupled with an honest repentance when we fail to give him even that.

So when God confronts us with our sin, we're not to blunt the edge of the rebuke by hiding behind the fact that we can't be sinless. God might say, "Sinless? You think at this stage of the game I'm asking you to be sinless? Have a bit of sense! I want you to love me, to give me a cheerful submission, to give me what, with my help, you're well capable of. Because it's sinners I love, I accept the realizable best rather then the unattainable ideal. Sinlessness is for another time and other circumstances. In the meantime love me as I've asked you to.[5]

"Let me deal with your sins, let me worry about the origin of sin, let me—since I have the wisdom and knowledge necessary for the task—let me do the tricky analyzing and searching out of the roots and tendrils of sin, the essence and nature of sin. Leave it to me to obliterate it, root and branch, and redeem everyone from it. In the meantime, don't analyze it so much. Denounce it and love me. Don't follow it's labyrinthine ways or try to ferret out its hidden forms; there are too many open sewers and recognizable wrongs you need to expose, to live down and leave behind, without your having to hunt the rare species. Renounce the obvious and love one another.

"Remember who I am, love and respect me for who I am, and as a consequence, love one another since I love each of you. See yourselves as loved by me and live accordingly. See your brothers and sisters and the whole world as loved by me and let that be your guide. You can make too much of sin and too little of life!"

But there is a spooky side to this. In confronting us with our sin, God says: "It's bad beyond your imagining. It's evil beyond your ability to grasp. It's worse than you know, and what you call its horror is the mask it wears to hide its true hideousness."

Sin is nothing to smile about. When we cherish what we're disgusted by, when we exalt what we damn, when we pay dearly for what we know is less than worthless, when we woo what violates us, when we're proud of what utterly shames us, when we whisper invitations to what we bar iron doors against—when we respond in all these ways to sin, we begin to sense what a deadly mutant we're facing. We invite it into our lives and still think we're normal. In the end, sin isn't only a spiritual mystery, it's spiritual lunacy.

In confronting us with sin, God doesn't mean to leave the impression that sin is the ultimate reality. It's no such thing. Even here we must remember that God alone is sovereign, and he alone must have center stage. Our minds should not be ceaselessly on our sin.

God hasn't obliterated the universe because his creation has rebelled, but that's only because of his love for humanity. Still, the love of God is more than a match for sin. Sin is strong, but God's love is stronger. Sin multiplies, but the grace of God more than overwhelms it. The last word is with God!

God's confronting us with our sin is not the same as damning us for it. Confrontation is part of his life-giving procedure. It's part of his calling us up to better things. It's part of his honoring us and assuring us that sin can be beat. It's one of his ways of saying we matter supremely to him; he *bothers!* He's there confronting our sins, hating them, delivering us from them, and promising that one day—one bright, blessed, glorious day—by his grace and goodness, we'll be done with them forever.

24

THE GOD WHO
HONORS US

The safest road to Hell is the gradual one—
the gentle slope, soft underfoot, without sudden turnings,
without milestones, without signposts.

C. S. LEWIS, *THE SCREWTAPE LETTERS*

To his eternal glory and praise, God doesn't take himself *too* seriously. Of all the beings we can imagine, no one would have the right to be self-absorbed and filled with pride as God would, but he lives so well with his matchless majesty and incomparable holiness that he is free to love, with joyful abandon, sinful humans—free to love us with pure love and without contempt. And he does!

To weak and sinful Israel, he proclaims:

> I will put my dwelling place among you, and I will not
> abhor you. I will walk among you and be your God,
> and you will be my people. I am the LORD your God,
> who brought you out of Egypt so that you would no
> longer be slaves to the Egyptians; I broke the bars of

your yoke and enabled you to walk with heads held
high. (Leviticus 26:11-13)

We need to begin where the text begins—with God. It is *God*
who does the putting, the walking, the bringing out, the breaking, the
enabling, and the nonabhorring. Israel didn't make herself God's
dwelling place, didn't elect herself as God's people, didn't make God
to be God. Israel didn't rescue herself from Egypt and enable her
people to walk with heads held high. The initiative, grace, and power
is God's from beginning to end.

God honors us by simply wanting to live with us. That itself
marks us as something special to him. If we saw Prince Charles or the
president of the United States stoop to pick something up off of
the street, wouldn't that object, whatever it turned out to be, now
have great significance? Wouldn't we all wonder what it was that so
interested a president or one of the royal family? Sinners or not, God
seeks entrance into our lives. The fact that he chooses to dwell with us
does us a great honor indeed.

But God is forever calling us "up," and this too honors us greatly.
If we were the slugs some well-intentioned people claim we are, leaving a slimy trail everywhere we crawl, would God place such astonishing faith in us? No one should suggest we are worthwhile without
God, nor should anyone underestimate the power of sin, but that's
only one part of the picture. Since God is always with us and enabling
us, we shouldn't speak or act with contempt about others. Curl our lip
at people long enough, and not only will we suffer loss, they'll begin
to believe us. Ask nothing of people, and they'll sink to a lower level.

If God calls us to goodness and gallantry, we should gladly accept what that implies: We *can* rise. There's a potential in us—a capacity for wondrous living—that we need to recognize and call on. Yes, God did the enabling, but he expected the Israelites to *walk* as befitted free men and women. He came to dwell with them to honor them; to *make* them something as well as *give* them something.

God told the Israelites, "I will not abhor you" (Leviticus 26:11). Our inner dignity rises when someone chooses to be our companion; chooses us and so makes us feel there's something of worth in us or that there *could be* something of worth in us. If that person, knowing us for what we are, shows us that they believe in us, then maybe we can rise above our sinful self-loathing that cripples and paralyzes us and move on to spiritual and moral maturity. Christ never spoke of people with utter contempt; it isn't like him. It's arrogant and completely destructive.

If we only knew how easy it is to crush a human heart with scorn, maybe we wouldn't be so quick to do so. And if we could see how people, given loving support and challenge, respond to the upward call, we might change our approach from cheap contempt to costly involvement. We might begin to ask more of them rather than less.

In the movie *Good Will Hunting*, Will Hunting is a mathematical genius with potential beyond imagining. His best friend, Chuckie, would lie down in front of a train for him. Chuckie believes Will is burying himself when he should be soaring. On the building site, during a break, the question arises about what Will's future holds. Will says he's going to live his life right there in the neighborhood, get married, and raise kids. Chuckie tells him: "Look, you're my best friend, so don't take this the wrong way. In twenty years if you're still living here, coming over to my house, watching the Patriot games, still working in construction—I'll kill you."

"What are you talking about?" Will grunts.

"You've got something none of us—"

And before he can go on, the irritated Will butts in, "Come on, why's it always this, 'I owe it to myself to do this or that'; what if I don't want—"

And now Chuckie butts in: "No, no, you don't owe it to *yourself*, you owe it to *me*. 'Cuz tomorrow I'm gonna wake up, and I'll be fifty, and I'll still be doing this...stuff. You're sitting on a winning lottery ticket and too much of a [jerk] to do something about it. I'd do anything to have what you've got.... It'd be an insult to us if you're still here in twenty years. Hanging around here is a waste of your time."

The genius snaps back, "You don't know that!" and they verbally spar for a moment.

"I don't know that?"

"You don't know that!"

"Oh...I don't know that? Let me tell you what I *do* know—d'you know what the best part of my day is? It's for about ten seconds, from when I pull up to the curb and get up to your door and knock on it. 'Cuz I think, maybe I'll get up to your door and knock on it, and you won't be there. No good-bye, no see you later, no nothin'...you just left. I know *that!*"

Even Chuckie knew that great potential shouldn't be squandered. God has equipped his children, equipped us to be women and men against the darkness, equipped us to live in and beat the wilderness. We're equipped because we have known and know the grace of God, which alone is sufficient for us. Many who don't know God have dropped out of the pursuit of noble living and don't want to bother; some even pride themselves in it. But there are those who listen to us and can't help wondering why we're as tasteless as egg whites and as flat as a day-old glass of Coke. They get glimpses now and then of what our story means, or should mean, and they think, *If it's true, why are they—?* In some real sense, it's an insult *to the world* when we fritter away our lives in boredom, setting our hearts on trivial things.

Apparently it's not just people who get fed up with the humdrum when gallant and exciting lives are a real possibility. I've been told on good authority that a boy camel was talking to his dad about this very thing. The conversation my source overheard went like this:

> SON: Dad, these two big humps on our backs, what are they for?
>
> DAD: Well, there's not a lot of food in the vast deserts we travel in, so we're able to store up a lot of food in these humps of ours. It's in the form of fat, you see.
>
> SON: That's marvelous. So what about these eyelashes. They're so heavy and thick. What's that all about?
>
> DAD: Yes, they are, aren't they? Well, in the desert we get these incredibly strong winds, and half the desert seems to be flying through the air. And the speed of that flying sand is dangerous. Others aren't as well-equipped as we are. We just shut these big heavy lids and clamp down these magnificent eyelashes, and—bingo!—we're safe.

SON: Can you beat that! Then these feet of ours. It
       seems like we have a double-helping, all sponge
       and spread. What are these for?

DAD: Deserts are incredibly dangerous places. It isn't
       hard for men and animals, like horses and cattle,
       to get swallowed up in that sand. Not us; we have
       these big feet so we won't go under and suffocate.

SON: Well, we're something else, aren't we, Pop? Just
       one more question—with all this equipment,
       what are we doing in the San Diego Zoo?

Modernist preacher Harry Emerson Fosdick insisted that Christ came not only to convict us of our sins, but to convict us of our possibilities. He was right! C. S. Lewis illustrates this truth in *The Screwtape Letters* when he has Screwtape urge his nephew, Wormwood, to foster *nothing* in the people he was tempting.

> "Nothing is very strong," says Screwtape, "strong
> enough to steal away a man's best years not in sweet
> sins but in a dreary flickering of the mind over it
> knows not what and knows not why…in drumming
> of fingers and clicking of heels, in whistling tunes he
> does not like."[1]

Of course, not everyone wants the rich and glorious life-filled life. But countless people wish to see strong goodness lived out before them. They feel the deep need to see that goodness is possible. They need to see believers knocked down for a worthwhile cause—down but not out, back on their feet again, *refusing* to concede defeat.

They need to see this in others because they've given up on themselves. They've concluded that authentic life is an endangered species, if still alive at all. They're slaves at the altar of the great god *Nothing*. They're crawling around the shrines of Narcissus and need someone to get them off their bellies or knees. They'd like to walk with their heads held high.

In Robert Browning's *Pompilia* the central character is dying, reflecting on her short life, wrestling with mystery about God, but rejoicing at the thought of a certain friend who made the difference. In closing she says:

> *Through such souls alone*
> *God stooping shows sufficient of His light*
> *For us in the dark to rise by. And I rise.*[2]

We see this illustrated in life and literature all the time, don't we? In the movie *The Natural,* Roy Hobbs is a good boy who becomes a good man. His first love is a girl and then comes baseball. He leaves the love of his life and heads for the city lights to make his name with a major baseball team, but as he put it, he "got sidetracked." As an older, better man he reappears, still a fantastic hitter and pitcher. With his decency and skill, he influences his struggling team to greater performances, greater integrity, and a championship. Again he gets sidetracked. The moral tone of his life diminishes, his playing skill is badly affected, and life takes a dive.

As he waits for the last ball from the pitcher, the ball that will strike him out—out of the game and out of real life—he looks toward the crowd and sees a familiar and beloved face. It's her, after all the years, standing while everyone else is sitting, smiling in his direction, willing him on. Something happens inside the man, a new purpose to live, a new strength, to see it through with honor. Somehow that makes a difference to his eye. He hits a massive home run.

Later, he's very ill in hospital, and she comes to visit him, to lift his heart and tell him of her continued love down through the years. He asks her, "That day in Chicago, why did you stand up?" She said, "I didn't want to see you fail."

I love those scenes, for they remind me of so many people who were *always* present in my life, and not only at my failures. They came to stay and in staying made it easier for me to rise again when I fell. They didn't come just to rebuke and heap scorn, they came to offer warmth, intimacy, and costly commitment, enabling me to succeed in some ways. They came in the name of God and stayed through all my life because they didn't want to see me fail. And in knowing them, I'm reminded of God who comes never to leave us, because he doesn't want to see us fail. He wants to help us to live royally and with honor. He won't leave us alone, is always prodding and demanding, sometimes chastising but never degrading, never isolating, never vengeful.

He wants us to walk with our heads held high.

25

THE GOD WHO
FORGIVES OUR SIN

And the blood of Jesus, his Son, purifies us from all sin.

1 JOHN 1:7

"I'm willing to forgive all your sins," God teaches us, "but you must at least be willing to confess there's something that needs to be forgiven."

God help us, we're so busy explaining why we sin that we sometimes forget that we've sinned. It's our parents, you see, or our environment, our culture, our peers and fears, our doubts and complexes; this is where all the trouble lies. By the time we're finished, we've explained why we had no choice but to sin, and so sin has vanished—we're not at all responsible. We have too much to say for ourselves!

But one of the purposes of the curse, one of the functions of the wilderness is to expose our sinning for what it is so that forgiveness can become possible. The shriek and bedlam of a world in turmoil functions to silence us, to generate a humble confession of dire need. It shuts our mouths so that we won't have too much to say for ourselves.

John Watson spoke of our wordiness in his lovely book *Beside the Bonnie Brier Bush,* when he tells of the approaching death of the old doctor, William MacLure, who had ministered to the townspeople for more than forty years. The Scottish community of Drumtochty saw the old man's health failing and conspired to pay him extra attention, for despite his rough tongue and manners he was greatly loved. It was a bitter December Sunday when Patrick Drumsheugh, a friend since childhood, paid the doctor a visit. He was shocked at how weak the old man had become and was shaken even more when the doctor asked him to spend the night and be with him at the end. Drumsheugh tried to talk him out of such thoughts, but the old man knew what he knew.

They talked for hours, more tenderly than they ever had before, now that both friends knew the end was nearing. The doctor confessed to getting drowsy and said he would soon not be able to follow the conversation, but he asked his friend to read a piece from the Bible, from his mother's Bible. He said to Drumsheugh, "Ye 'ill need tae come close tae the bed, for a'm no hearin' or seein' sae weel as a' wes when ye cam."

Patrick put on his glasses, looking for a piece of Scripture that would give comfort at a time like this, and he chose John 14, "in my Father's house there are many mansions." He told the dying doctor that his own mother always wanted that read when she was ailing, but the old man stopped him. "It's a bonnie word, an' yir mither wes a sanct; but it's no for the likes o' me. It's ower gude; a' daurna tak it."

So he told his friend to close the Bible and then let it fall open by itself. It would open, said the dying man, at the place where he'd been reading every night for a month. His friend did what he asked and the book opened at the parable of the Pharisee and the publican. Drumsheugh read, "And the publican, standing afar off, would not lift up so much as his eyes to heaven, but smote upon his breast, saying, God be merciful to me a sinner."

The old doctor said, "That micht hae been written for me, Patrick, or ony ither auld sinner that hes feenished his life, an' hes naething tae say for himsel."

There it is! *Has nothing to say for himself.* No explanations, no denials, no excuses; no extenuating circumstances or sob stories; no bitter recriminations or long list of good deeds done that might outweigh the bad. When face to face with the holy and loving Father— nothing to say for himself.

When the disciples returned from their home mission travels, thrilled to heaven to tell Christ of demons expelled and lives healed, he gives them something to ponder. "Do not rejoice that the spirits submit to you, but rejoice that your names are written in heaven" (Luke 10:20).

Didn't they have reason to rejoice in the powers that God had given them to effect such changes? Yes! Yes! Yes! But so that they wouldn't short-circuit things, Christ urged them to rejoice in what these powers *meant:* that God had invaded the world in Jesus Christ and had brought life with him. He wanted his disciples to see beyond the signs to what they signified. He wanted them to see themselves as part of redeemed humanity, part of the forgiven inheritors of life. They had more than God's gifts—they had God and life with him in Jesus Christ!

A poet told the story of a long-forgotten battlefield and a day on which a savage engagement had been fought. That evening two believers moved among the many dead and dying, speaking words of comfort, offering guidance, making promises to carry messages, and speaking of the sacrifice of Jesus Christ.

They came across one young man who lay alone, white and still, his helmet fallen from his head, but his hand still grasping his broken sword. Thinking he was dead, they were moving on. That's when they heard a soft sigh. The soldier was alive, but barely. So kneeling down they whispered to him, gently and earnestly, things about Christ. How amazed they were when his bloodless lips moved and spoke a gentle, "Hush!" After that it looked like life had gone, but when the men whispered to him, the dying soldier, with great effort, earnestly whispered, "Hush! for the angels call the muster roll! I wait to hear my name!"

> *They spoke no more.*
> *What need to speak again? for now full well*
> *They knew on whom his dying hopes were fixed,*
> *And what his prospects were. So, hushed and still,*
> *They, kneeling, watched.*
>
> *And presently a smile,*
> *As of the most thrilling and intense delight,*
> *Played for a moment on the soldier's face,*
> *And with his one last breath he whispered, "Here!"*[1]

To hear God's word of acceptance, when fully alive or on our deathbed—that above all things we strain to hear: "Well done, good and faithful servant.... Enter into the joy of your lord" (Matthew 25:21, NKJV).

All that Israel saw foreshadowed in the tabernacle was fully spelled out when God tabernacled with us in Jesus the Christ. Israel knew about forgiveness, because there in the middle of the wilderness—a wilderness that spoke of their unbelief and the curse that accompanies it—*there* God gave them the blood on their altars to make atonement.[2]

The vast wilderness of all the ages thunders that a holy God recoils against our human rebellion; it bears witness to the awfulness of our treason—if we hadn't rebelled there'd be no wilderness. But Israel's wilderness contained things that proclaimed a larger story and told other truths that we too desperately need to hear. The very existence of the entire tabernacle structure—its sacrificial system, silver bases (sockets) made of redemption money, the ark of the covenant, the mercy seat, the Day of Atonement, and other ordinances—all these and more bore witness to the possibility and reality of forgiveness, because God chose to be present with humanity.

Today the New Testament church would join with the Old Testament church in proclaiming the same truth. We'd point to ordinances like baptism, the Lord's Supper, the proclaimed Word, and the like, all of which bear witness to the presence of the forgiving and life-giving Lord whose blood was shed as an atoning sacrifice for the whole world (1 John 2:1-2).

This is profoundly great news for those who take sin seriously. In Jesus Christ our sins are dealt with, not simply in ones and twos, but the whole. Sins of the night and day, sins of speech and thought, sins of doing and not doing, sins of the flesh and mind, secret sins, open sins, darling sins, respectable sins and gross, sins of eyes and ears, showy sins and subtle sins, unexpected sins and the parasitic sins that dog our feet. Strong, victorious, strutting sins that have laughed at humanity down the ages. All—all are dealt with.

Wasn't it Martin Luther who, in a fit of deep depression, seemed to see Satan making a record of his sins on the wall? The list was long and varied, it filled the room and it seemed that it would fill the world as the pitiless adversary, rejoicing in his work, tried to kill the heart of the sinner. And aren't we told that Luther prayed and then, looking steadily at his grinning enemy said, "You have forgotten just one thing!"

"And what's that?" the World Hater asked.

"Take your pen once more and write across it all: 'The blood of Jesus Christ, His Son, cleanses us from all sin.'"

If you had said to Moses: "Look around you at the desolation and look at this sinful people. What gives you your confidence?" Moses could have pointed to the tabernacle and said, "God's loving presence is with us, even here." And if you'd asked the grinning and transformed Peter what was thrilling the heart out of him, he'd have said, "I've seen him, and he has forgiven me. Can you believe it?" And the wilderness blossoms and becomes a park filled with adventure.

Having said all that and believing it's built on the immovable and massive truths about God and his grace, now and then I wonder why he would bother with us in light of our sinfulness and our shallowness.

I know that we can't fully appreciate the gift of forgiveness, and I know it because we don't and can't grasp the nature of our sin and the long, long patience and the deep, deep love of God. But isn't it startling how blasé we can be about it? Sometimes we react to forgiveness as if God were a friend paying for our lunch. "How kind of you," we say, and we mean it. But we aren't dumbfounded by it, and that itself is astonishing.

P. T. Forsyth, Great Britain's apostle of the holiness of God, raged against our tendency to receive forgiveness so calmly, raged against our minimizing our sin as though it were of some consequence but not something to get overwrought about. He scathed our refusal to face the true nature of our wickedness:

> What ails us is not limitation but transgression, not
> poverty but alienation. It is the breach of communion
> that is the trouble—the separation, the hostility....
> There is a huge dislocation. There is that in us and in
> our sin which is in its very essence intractable to all the
> processes of a reconciling idea; something which, to
> the end, by its very nature, refuses to be taken up as a
> factor into the largest and most comprehensive proces-
> sion of divine action; something which can never be
> utilized, but can only be destroyed in a mortal moral
> war; something which, if God cannot kill it, must be
> the death of God. And as a race we are not even stray
> sheep, or wandering prodigals merely; we are rebels
> taken with weapons in our hands.
>
> Our supreme need from God, therefore, is not
> the education of conscience, nor the absorption of our
> sin, nor even our reconcilement alone, but our redemp-
> tion. It is not cheer that we need but salvation; not
> help but rescue; not a stimulus but a change; not tonics
> but life.[3]

If we view humanity as one rebellious family and believe what Forsyth said to be so, how can we but stand in wonder at God's holy grace? If not now, we will later.

> *O Lord, how can you love humanity so? When we so love our sins, nurture and admire them; when we justify our coldness toward you and others; when we watch unmoved the world's great wrongs and great pain; when we're so self-serving and our repentance needs to be repented of; when we seek out evil as you seek out ways to forgive and heal—how can you love us so? How can it be that you are incomparable in your delight to forgive sins, you who are holy beyond our imagining? Even so, for Christ's dear sake, we tremblingly rejoice that forgiveness is full and free to us though so costly to you. And we thank you as much as sinners like us can, with all our hearts.*

Speechless!

26

THE GOD WHO
MUST BE CENTER

Love the Lord your God with all your heart and with all your soul
and with all your mind. This is the first and greatest commandment.

MATTHEW 22:37-38

If we'd flown over the ancient Israelite camp, we would have seen thousands of tents arranged around a central, larger tent. North, south, east, and west we'd see groups of tents belonging to the various tribes in their assigned places. Everything would face the center of the camp where the tabernacle stood, the place in which the God of Israel dwelled.

The very physical structure of the camp reflected this truth about God: He can't accept—nor should he be offered—any place but center in the life, affection, will, and worship of his people. He seeks our highest good and knows that can only come when we place him at the center.

It wasn't just the structure of the tabernacle that made this truth clear. Not long before he died, Moses warned Israel against making idols, "For the LORD your God is a consuming fire, a jealous God" (Deuteronomy 4:24). And listen to this for bluntness. God is speaking to Israel and telling her he is making a covenant with her so she's not to worship any other god, "for the LORD, whose name is Jealous, is a jealous God" (Exodus 34:14).

The way we think about jealousy makes us uneasy before passages like this. We want to dismiss the image of God as a husband who, every time his wife steps out of the house, asks a hundred probing questions when she returns. We don't want to think of God as someone who smolders if we come to love someone very deeply. Just the same, these passages must mean something.

The admonition, "Don't give to others what belongs to me" seems plain enough, until we press it for meaning. Are we sure we know what belongs to God and not to others? Might we withhold things from others that God wants us to give? In terms of husband-and-wife relationships, we feel sure that we should draw some clear lines, but that doesn't answer all the serious questions.

Moses had been God's spokesman for the people from the beginning, but he needed others to share the prophetic load, so the Lord put his Spirit on forty others who prophesied—outside the camp. They prophesied once, which marked them as God's chosen, I suppose. But two of the forty continued to speak within the confines of the camp, and Joshua heard about it. He went to Moses and urged him to stop them because he felt it would undermine Moses' authority with the people. Moses' response is this: "Are you jealous for my sake? I wish that all the LORD's people were prophets and that the LORD would put his Spirit on them!" (Numbers 11:29). Joshua's jealousy was triggered by a situation that he judged as harmful, but it was misplaced because what had happened hurt neither Moses nor the people.

Every time the Bible speaks about God as jealous, those he loves are in a dangerous situation. Seeking after other gods, worshiping idols, despising the covenant God had made with Israel—all would destroy those he loved and interfere with his universal purpose for humanity, our redemption. Such actions take what is worthless and puts it in the place of the irreplaceable God. This plain self-destruction insults God's majesty.

So God's jealousy is a holy refusal to be rejected. And it comes at a critical point and relates to something very basic. We're not talking about fine-tuning the relationship between God and his people; it's a matter of infidelity and walking away from God to serve someone or something else.

Frank Boreham, the prolific Australian author and preacher, told of his friend John Broadbanks and his wife, Lilian. Their little girl, Myrtle, was the cream in their coffee, their warmth in the cold; she brought sunshine and enthusiasm into their lives by the bucketful. How...they...loved...the child. Then she became very ill, and they were sure she would die. The world fell in around them. They cried, unable to stop, begged God for her life, and moped through the long days and nights.

Lilian had visions of clinging to her daughter's coffin and wailing without comfort for the rest of her life. Then her conscience smote her, and she began to think of hymns such as William Cowper's "O for a Closer Walk with God," which says:

> *The dearest idol I have known,*
> *What e'er that idol be,*
> *Help me to tear it from Thy throne,*
> *And worship only thee.*

She whispered her fears to John, who had not long before preached on the sin of idolatry. They talked it out over a period of days while the child's life hung in the balance, and they both concluded that their fierce and tender love for their little Myrtle didn't make God jealous at all, not at all.

Could God look with anger and envy at a father and mother who adored the gentle baby he had given them? Perhaps. But what had Myrtle's arrival done to the Broadbank house? John verbalized it for both of them one evening when he said: "Well, Lilian, have we given God cause for jealousy? Has the coming of Myrtle into our lives led us to love Him less—or more? I think since Myrtle came our hearts have been softened and sweetened, and we have felt more thankful and trustful than ever. And if that's so, Lilian, then Myrtle's no idol. She has not weaned us away from God; she has bound us more securely to Him."

If a relationship softens our hearts toward God, deepens our gratitude, and strengthens our purpose to please him, it doesn't matter how deeply we love that person; God is not offended, he isn't jealous. In cases like that, we don't worship the gift, we adore God for the gift, and he loves the other through us. We are his gift to them. God's being central need not make us uneasy, but it will encourage and enable us to examine our lives and see to it that they're shaped and purposed to his glory.

However, we're not to think, *Well, it's good that we have that out of the way. It's good that now we know God isn't really a jealous God.* We know no such thing! *Since we've no intention of bowing down to idols, we can relax now and get back to our "happy hour" at church.* We can do no such thing! Finding deep pleasure in the presence of the Lord is one thing, crossing the line from a reverent intimacy with God to become what Annie Dillard calls "cheerful, brainless tourists on a packaged tour of the Absolute"[1] is something else.

If the God who buried Egypt is central in our lives, he will affect our worship and how we construct that worship. Our worship might generate joy and pleasure in us, but it won't be entertainment or a carnival—it'll be worship. It might bring deep pleasure, but it might also bring a sharp pang of conviction that leaves us distressed rather than comforted, uncertain rather than assured. Our worship will stress God's holy majesty and glory because he's worthy of it and because puny humans become more pathetic when we can see nothing higher than ourselves.

The God who'd had enough of Sodom and Gomorrah is in earnest to get us out of our sin; he's earnest about loving and redeeming a world at great cost to himself and us. If we make God central to us and throw in our lot with him, to achieve his purposes, who he is and what he's after will shape our worship, but I doubt if it'll turn it into a lighthearted evening at the local talent show.

God wants our *worship!* This is why everything in Israel's camp faced the central tabernacle, which was the focal point of their worship. Everything about the tabernacle, including the priesthood and the sacrificial system, proclaimed loud and clear the importance of worship to God, the importance of making *God* center.

Worship kept Israel's eyes focused on God rather than on themselves; focused on him rather than on their daily and necessary mundane operations. Worship kept them from falling into the habit of thinking there's nothing more to life than what they could see, eat, drink, or understand. It kept mystery alive. "Magic" filled the air when they looked and saw the Shekinah. Worship kept their eyes on Yahweh rather than other gods. The tabernacle, with its Holy of Holies and the ark of the covenant, reminded them of the covenant God had made with them and they with him. And how Israel responded to that covenant in their daily lives outside the tabernacle colored the worship conducted within the tabernacle.

Worship can be used to escape godly and righteous living, and Israel's prophets reminded a worshiping community that what God really wanted wasn't animal sacrifices and burning incense. What he wanted, they said, was lives of humility and kindness, lives of faithfulness to honorable commitments. And making him central in that way would enrich their worship and make it an authentic confession that God was at their heart. Karl Barth cleverly made this point when he said, "Christians go to church to make their last stand against God."[2] At times we'll give God anything, even worship, to keep from giving him what he wants. William Willimon, minister at the University Church at Duke, follows Barth in this by saying, "While the stated aim of Sunday worship...may be 'meeting,' it can also be a time in which we use a series of well-defined acts to avoid meeting God, ourselves, or others."[3]

If we avoid God by making something or someone else the center of life, we're altogether missing the mark. There is no sense in saying that truth doesn't matter, that worship is irrelevant, that doctrine is of no consequence, that uprightness is optional or that community is even more so. None of that would be true. But if all the truth, all the behavior, all the worship, all the doctrinal truth is not in the service of a vital relationship with a personal God, it falls dead in its tracks. It not only cheats God of what he wants, it cheats us of what he wants for us and what we in our saner moments want for ourselves—a relationship with a person.

John Oxenham expressed it clearly for us.

> *Not what, but whom I do believe,*
> *That in my darkest hour of need,*
> *Hath comfort that no mortal creed*
> *To mortal man may give;*
> *Not what, but whom!*
> *For Christ is more than all the creeds,*
> *And his full life of gentle deeds*
> *Shall all the creeds outlive.*
> *Not what, but whom!*
> *Who walks beside me in the gloom?*
> *Who shares the burden wearisome?*
> *Who all the dim way doth illume,*
> *And bids me look beyond the tomb*
> *The larger life to live?—*
> *Not what do I believe,*
> *But whom!*
> *Not what*
> *But whom!*[4]

27

THE GOD WHO
GIVES SABBATH

Anyone who enters God's rest also rests from his own work,
just as God did from his.

HEBREWS 4:10

Wilbur Rees had his eye on the feverish and restless modern spirit that wants to fix everything when he has one of his characters say,

> Here I sit in my director's chair. What an intolerable
> role. "You there! Your makeup is on too thick! Tell the
> lighting man to tone down the flood. Get those extras
> out of here! Okay, everybody quiet." It's no easy job to
> be the director, to make everybody over a little bit, to
> change people, to manipulate. I stumble to my room
> for a bit of a rest and read the nameplate on my door.
> "Almighty God."[1]

The wilderness cured Israel of the notion of their own godhood and self-sufficiency. With its unblinking stare, the wilderness proclaimed Israel's vulnerability and their helplessness in the same way that a cancer-riddled body or the crumpled and lifeless victim of a hit-and-run proclaims ours. The wilderness invariably kept the children of Israel under threat, withholding water and food and subjecting them to howling winds, blistering heat in the day, and freezing cold at night. Had they been alone in the desert they would have been in ceaseless anxiety: "Where's the food going to come from? Where are we going to get water? How will we clothe ourselves?"

When George Macdonald spoke of "the God-denying look of things," he had situations like the wilderness in mind; but when he calmly announced the Sabbath, God defied the wilderness, he defied the world that would have driven Israel and us to feverish and vain activity.

When the Israelites were in the wilderness, God gave them the Sabbath as a confession of their utter dependence on him. They didn't get their food and drink by their wisdom or expertise, their hustling or searching. God instructed them to rest on the seventh day of the week as a visible and national affirmation that the same God who created the world in six days was the one who had brought them into the wilderness and was providing for them there.

> Remember the Sabbath day by keeping it holy. Six
> days you shall labor and do all your work, but the
> seventh day is a Sabbath to the LORD your God. On
> it you shall not do any work.... For in six days the
> LORD made the heavens and the earth, the sea, and
> all that is in them, but he rested on the seventh day.
> (Exodus 20:8-11)

For six days, out of the original void-filled formlessness, God created harmony and teeming life before he "rested" in satisfied joy. The Jewish week was structured as God's creation week had been, thus retelling the creation story of Genesis 1. By perpetually imitating their Lord, the Israelites proclaimed him as sole creator and provider for the whole world. If you had asked an enlightened Jew why he worked six days and didn't work on the seventh day, he would have told you, "We're acting out the creation week. The seventh day declares that nothing needs to be added because God has provided everything. When we rejoice and feast on the Sabbath, we bear witness that we aren't our own saviors; we confess that we live in and through the completed work of God; we insist that we don't depend on ourselves to sustain ourselves."

Men and women who work in prospering countries may still acknowledge this, of course, but a nation in a wilderness? This is a confession indeed, and one Israel had no option but to make. The Sabbath proclaims its message anywhere, but it has an added power when it is lived out by a nation in a desert. By a nation that *conquered* the desert!

God goes to great pains to make the truth of the Sabbath stick. He speaks to a nation that is grumbling about the starvation that faces them, and he promises them manna. But he promises them manna in connection with the Sabbath. Exodus 16 tells us that each day the Israelites were to go out and gather the manna according to their needs, but the Lord himself keeps control of the supply of bread, not Israel. Those who gathered more than an omer (about two quarts) per person found they had no more, and those who gathered less found they had enough. They were not to keep the manna until the next morning, and those who did found it wormy. They were to gather double the amount on the sixth day, and on the seventh they were to rest. Those who didn't trouble to gather enough manna on the sixth day found there was none on the Sabbath. In all this, God was telling Israel that *he* was the provider. The rules that governed the bread were designed to make that clear, and they were given in connection with the giving of the Sabbath.

All this might suggest that the Sabbath was a day of gloom and arbitrary regulations, but in Jewish tradition, the Sabbath is no day to lie around listlessly. It's a day of joy, the reading of Scriptures on creation and redemption; it's a day of eating and pleasure. The Jewish tradition is that each family has two loaves of bread on the table, which speak of the double portion of manna that was supplied in the wilderness. They end the day with a little service of sadness that the day is departing. America's most prolific rabbi, Jacob Neusner, said this of Sabbath observance: "Those who compare the Sabbath of Judaism to the somber, supposedly joyless Sunday of the Calvinists know nothing of what the Sabbath has meant and continues to mean to Jews."[2] The Sabbath speaks not of joyless dependence but of glad-hearted trust, of assurance, and confidence that the whole issue of life lies ultimately in the hands of a God who is more than able and willing.

And the message of God's Sabbath gift to Israel is just as needed now in a world as filled with heat and fever as any desert. In a world of bedlam, where we're running backward and forward, piling up debts, trying to keep up with the Joneses, working every hour we can get—in a world like ours, we need the message of the gift of Sabbath. *God* provides! In lives without rest, hearts without peace, and days ceaselessly filled with the need to control, the Sabbath says, "Turn it loose! Reflect on God's promises and his faithful adequacy and let his peace surround you."

The message of the Sabbath is part of the cure for all our fever—

even religious fever—in which people attempt to *do* enough to earn God's favor or to stay on his good side. And we hear a lot of ministers nurturing this as they go on about the need for the church to be adequate for God. But we're not to forget that *in the wilderness* God called Israel to proclaim his complete adequacy and providence, while they stood by, panting in helplessness. We're not to panic, nor are we ever to think that God needs us to sustain him.

God help us, sometimes we have no sense of our weakness and limits, because we have everything under control. Scads of well-skilled staff keep the religious machine oiled and running smoothly, with programs and goals all in place. We've no sense of desperation; no sense of the magnitude of the task before us because we've shrunk it to manageable proportions and our "success" hides our failure to take on the full job. We don't fail at the full-blooded attempt because we're too busy with the trimmed-down version. The apostle Paul groans, and stunned by the magnitude of the task, he asks us, "Who is sufficient for these things?" (2 Corinthians 2:16, NKJV), and our hands and heads shoot up, "We are! We are!" But we never were nor will we ever be. The good news is, we don't have to be; we don't carry God, he carries us! Isaiah 46:1-2 offers us this:

> Bel bows down, Nebo stoops low;
>> their idols are borne by beasts of burden.
> The images that are carried about are burdensome,
>> a burden for the weary.
> They stoop and bow down together;
>> unable to rescue the burden,
>> they themselves go off into captivity.

Here's the picture. Babylon is about to fall to the Medo-Persians, and its leaders are anxious that the gods don't fall into the hands of the enemy. The huge gates of Babylon swing open and out come massive wagons, drawn by scores of powerful oxen, with brawny men alongside the wagons, supporting them. Imagine donkeys tied together in groups to help take the weight, and see them stumbling under the heavy load. Listen to the wheels of the creaking wagons, unable to carry the load one moment longer, and see them falling apart and the whole burden tumbling onto the ground—gargantuan idols sprawling face-down in the dust. That's the picture.

And God would want us to ask, "What's wrong with that picture?" He himself answers the question with a question. Shouldn't gods sustain people? He wants Israel to remember that they didn't carry him. He'd brought them forth, and it was he who'd sustained them from the beginning, and if they were to make it through to the end, it would be because he carried them.[3]

The other side of ignorantly claiming to have control is the hand-wringing we believers can fall into. Sometimes it's understandable, but sometimes it's a disgrace. If we hear someone prominent say he or she has time for God, we're comforted and assured, but when we hear others, celebrities maybe, or government officials, saying critical things, we're tempted to tremble. We hear of terrible court decisions and lament as though Christ were about to be dethroned. We see dwindling assemblies, saddening statistics about divorces or crimes, and fearfully we begin to hustle around in our wilderness to provide manna for God and so stave off his defeat. At times like this we know nothing of the Sabbath.

What if we heard God say: "So, the pagans are pounding at the doors of the church, and you're worrying about me? Wondering how you will keep me from going into captivity? Wondering if I can survive an insolent movie or a sports celebrity, a generation of arrogant scientists or a crew of silly government officials? You're going into panic because some flaky version of the Bible has just come out or a book that attacks me has been on the *New York Times* bestseller list for a year? You're worried that you might not be able to prop me up much longer? Try not to worry. Just relax and keep the Sabbath."

The sabbatical principle belongs to all those who have seen and believed in God. Wilderness conditions, external and internal, rage against the peace God grants to his people and offers to the whole wide world. But the God who created harmony and gave rest in the wilderness that Israel faced can create peace and harmony in a life, a church, a nation, and a whole world. Chaos in a life and in a world challenges that claim, but if we can remember that God *brought* Israel into the wilderness and *there* gave them Sabbath rest, maybe that truth can bring peace to our hearts and lives, individually and collectively.

28

THE GOD WHO
BRINGS US HOME

Praise be to the God and Father
of our Lord Jesus Christ!
In his great mercy he has given us
new birth into a living hope
through the resurrection of Jesus Christ
from the dead, and into an inheritance that can
never perish, spoil or fade—kept in heaven for you.

1 PETER 1:3-4

Since God has gone to such great lengths to get us home, wouldn't
you suppose that whatever he has in mind must be wonderful beyond
description? I mean, he wouldn't have subjected his beloved humanity
to such a severe wilderness if the pilgrimage was to end with an everlasting yawn or eternal boredom. There *must* be a glorious life ahead.
And this is what Paul has in mind when he dismisses the present suffering as something unworthy to be compared with the glory to be
revealed (Romans 8:18; 2 Corinthians 4:17). *The wilderness is not
forever!*

God is the one who will see us home, but the question is: The home he brings us to, is it worth all the trouble it takes to get there?

Irving Bacheller's *Eben Holden* tells the story of "Uncle" Eben, who takes an orphaned boy, Bill, on a great adventure and ends up in the lovely community of Paradise Valley under the warmth of David Brower's friendship. It's a marvelous book with marvelous characters, including old Doctor Bigsby.

One wintry day in thirty-below-zero weather, with the house creaking under the tight grip of the freezing cold, the doctor's horse and buggy came to a halt outside David's door. The old man was near death when they brought him in, but he recovered for a moment or two and talked about people who needed him to go tend to them. Then his big, generous heart gave out.

Brower and the company were lamenting the doctor's death when Uncle Eb said of the doctor:

"If a man oughter go t' Heaven, he had."

"Think he's in heaven?" Bill asked his uncle, and Eb said there was no doubt about it.

"What kind of a place do you think it is?" the boy asked.

Eben said: "To my way o' thinkin' it'll be a good deal like Dave Brower's farm—nice, smooth land and no stun on it, an' hills an' valleys an' white clover aplenty, an' wheat an' corn higher'n a man's head. No bull thistles, no hard winters, no narrer contracted fools; no long faces, an' plenty o' work. Folks sayin'

'How d'y do' 'stid o' 'goodbye,' all the while—comin'
'stid o' goin'. There's goin' t' be some kind o' fun there.
I ain' no idee what 'tis. Folks like it an' I kind o' believe
'at when God's gin a thing t' everybody he thinks
purty middlin' well uv it."[1]

I'm persuaded by Uncle Eb. If God thinks a thing's worth giving,
he must think "purty middlin' well uv it"; and if he thinks that well of
it, it must be really worth having. So heaven's worth looking forward to.

I don't doubt that there are mysteries about it all. For pity's sake,
there's mystery about where many of my socks go when they disap-
pear into the washing machine. What's so mysterious about there being
mysteries?

But for all that, I suspect that heaven is heaven because it confirms and eternalizes, purifies and magnifies all the lovely and wondrous things God has taught us to love and esteem here, in this phase
of living. And it's because such a home is ahead of us that the present
wilderness life is made more than bearable! Thoughts of home transform the wilderness.

G. A. Studdert Kennedy, a World War I chaplain, was a deeply
sensitive and high-strung man. He described the world created by
humans as:

> Sad as the winds that sweep across the ocean,
> Telling to earth the sorrow of the sea.
> Vain is my strife, just empty idle motion,
> All that has been is all there is to be.

I mention Kennedy because he was one of those who saw with special clarity life's great sorrows and humanity's great wrongs. Because this was so, he believed that hope-bringing truths should be spoken with some sense of realism. Preachers and churchgoing people spoke the word *peace* too glibly, and in irritation Kennedy wanted to know, "Where on earth has peace been ever found?"

But though despondency, born out of long experience with sufferers, tinged his realism, Kennedy was far from despair, because he believed God loved the human race and was working glory for himself and for them. Because he believed God loved the world, he knew that all the heartache and wickedness shouldn't and wouldn't have the last word. Love would!

There is a promise implicit in the truth of God's love for humanity: Things as they are cannot be the end. The transformed lives we see around us every day and the dramatic rescues of the derelicts offer us visible, though only partial, proofs of this. Yes, these and the hosts of lives kept from sinking into the depths of wickedness and cruelty. All these are partial but genuine proofs that the love of God has been let loose in the world and is doing its painfully costly work.

This kind of faith and experience led Paul to say, "He who began a good work in you will bring it to completion" (Philippians 1:6, RSV).

This led Australian preacher Frank Boreham to say a dishonorable God could not have made an honorable world, a deaf God could not have made a hearing world, and a loveless God could not have made a world with so much love in it. So if indeed God is love and that love is shown to us in Christ Jesus—a love that's reflected in countless lives in every generation—there must be more ahead than this; there must be better ahead than this! The staggering nature of God's love requires it.

The historian A. W. Momerie said that Pietro, the tyrannical duke of Florence, compelled Michelangelo to mold a statue out of snow, knowing that the Italian sun would melt it in an hour or two. It was a wanton waste of the genius's talent. How much greater a waste, says Momerie, if God should create man in his own image and allow him to rot in the tomb forever?

Paul said: "If only for this life we have hope in Christ, we are to be pitied more than all men" (1 Corinthians 15:19). In the light of the love of God in Jesus Christ, sorrow, loneliness, injustice, cruelty, oppression, sickness, suffering, and death *must* come to an end and *life* must continue, enriched and eternal! If God were not who he is and had not done what he has done, we could settle for less, could perhaps hide our disappointment and, in light of our sinfulness, be thankful that we are blessed at all. But it is *God* who won't allow us to settle for less! It is *God* who insists that our eyes haven't seen, our ears haven't heard, and our hearts can't imagine the glories that he has prepared for those who love him.[2]

Believe it. Our very failures and disappointments keep saying to us: "This? This is all that God has been bringing us to? This is the glorious completion for which he created us? And the sacrifice of Christ? This is what God has gone to all that agony and judgment for? His eternal love and holiness end here? No, not only is the present not the completion, for those who believe and rejoice in the love of the holy Father, it's the proof that it *isn't* the completion."

Some of us die young after a rich, full, and glorious life, but a host of us continue the grand walk in later years toward paradise with the full assurance that we haven't seen anything yet. So it's fitting for us to finish this study with Robert Browning's words in his poem "Rabbi Ben Ezra":

> *Grow old along with me!*
> *The best is yet to be,*
> *The best of life, for which the first was made;*
> *Our times are in His hand*
> *Who saith, "A whole I planned,*
> *Youth shows but half; trust God: see all nor be afraid!"*[3]

Questions for Group Discussion or Personal Reflection

1. W. M. Clow said: "Do you sometimes long for that simple and unquestioning faith in God's love which you had when you knelt at your mother's knee? That you cannot have. God has a better thing in store for you." How does that strike you? What faith is better than our childhood faith?

2. Why is the message of chapter 7, "Lizzie Eaton's Scales," especially important in a book like this?

3. What can we say in the face of biblical texts where God ordered the slaying even of little children? What are our options?

4. Does the truth that God is sovereign over all of creation mean there is no such thing as "chance" in our world? Or is God sovereign over the unpredictable (chance) part of the creation?

5. God does not originate sin nor does he approve it, but he is sovereign even over our sinfulness. Can you illustrate the truth of this with some big biblical events?

6. What does the author mean when he says that in the very same act men were murdering God's Son and God was sacrificing him?

7. Why wouldn't it be proper to say God *murdered* his Son?

8. Is it possible today for God to be sacrificing one of his children even as the murderer is murdering his child?

9. In chapter 4, "God's Curse and Little Children," the author says he doesn't believe the sickness or death of little children is their punishment for their sins (since they aren't guilty of any), but he believes they *share* the curse God brought on humanity because of its rebellion. Are these innocents in that respect bearing *our* sins?

10. What can you list that these suffering children teach us?

11. Only the suffering of Jesus Christ atones for sins, but it's true just the same that vicarious suffering is seen throughout life when others suffer on our behalf. In this respect, do you think it's true that a little child in its innocent suffering can say to us: "This is my body which is given for you"?

12. In the case of Joseph's going into Egypt, is this another case of sinners selling their brother and God putting his child to grief for redemptive purposes?

13. A Bible professor recently suggested that we shouldn't offer explanations about suffering since the Bible has already said enough.

He said that instead of talking, we should get involved in others' lives. How does that strike you? What strengths or weaknesses do you see in that perspective?

14. If it's true that God is subjecting humanity to such a *severe* mercy in order to redeem us, what can we infer about the future? And how does this implication about the future impact the present?

15. In the movie *Glory* (see pages 22-26), what things do the relationship between the colonel, Robert Gould Shaw, and his friend, Thomas, help us to grasp?

16. God placed Job on the ash heap, subjecting him to terrible suffering, because he was so proud of him. What does that sentence mean and how can you develop the thought?

17. Those who have no compassion for the hurting and who refuse to offer assistance are out of line. Those who are hard and can with ease withhold sympathy are unlike the Master. But if we never offer people a framework within which to work with their suffering, are we withholding strength from them?

18. This is a delicate question and needs delicate handling: Is it possible to weaken sufferers by *ceaselessly* sympathizing without ever calling for a gallant response to severe hardship?

19. Who do you know who suffers greatly but lifts your heart? (Develop your answer and say precisely why they do.)

20. If God wouldn't spare his own Son in his work of reconciling the world unto himself, should his children resent his putting them to grief if that is his will? (See Philippians 1:29 and 1 Peter 2:19-21.)

21. If God put his own Son to grief, subjecting him to the curse while loving him immeasurably, what implications does that have for his children in particular and humanity in general?

22. If God carries out his will through secondary agents, is it still the will of God being done?

23. Professor John C. L. Gibson said:

> We still find it exceedingly difficult to sanction
> the Old Testament's habitually robust habit of
> attributing evil to God's direct will. We prefer to
> avoid the issue by having the Devil, or even some
> impersonal force, perform the evil, and God simply
> permit it. But that is in theory only. What do we do
> in practice? When trouble comes our way we do not
> usually wonder what the Devil, or the principalities
> and powers, have to do with it, but in pain and
> perplexity we ask what God is up to. As in so many
> other spheres, our practice is perhaps more revealing
> than our theory.

How does that strike you? And why *do* we practice this? Be as honest as you can in explaining your answer.

24. Sin is not at all to be equated with suffering; they're not the same thing! How many ways can you make that clear?

25. A good surgeon will reluctantly inflict suffering, using sharp instruments to cut into someone. A man in the street may do the same thing to a passerby. Suffering is the result in both cases, but one is *sin* and the other is not. What makes the difference?

26. As it turned out, though he didn't know it, Job was fighting God's fight for him against all the forces of cynicism and darkness. Could that be true in your sufferings?

27. What made Moses' offer to Hobab (see pages 56-63) such a marvelous thing?

28. Do you know many non-Christians who are gallant in their hardships? Where do they get their strength?

29. Would you prefer to see your suffering in terms of a cup God asks humanity (and his children in particular) to drink, or see it as the result of mere bad luck or some freelance demonic thug who can do what he wants with whomever he wants?

30. If we pray for rain and it begins to rain, to whom do we give the credit? If it continues to rain and rain and rain and floods devastate homes, what do we say? Did God control the rain until there was enough and then some demon who has power over creation turn the showers into floods?

31. What was Satan confessing when he said to God, "Stretch out your hand and strike" (Job 1:11; 2:5)? In light of those two texts and Job 42:11, who stretched out his hand and struck Job?

32. Satan has power, but where does he get it? Satan has his own sinful agenda, but who is controlling it and using it?

33. Does Satan have control over creation so that he can, if he wishes, create tidal waves, earthquakes, tornadoes, and hurricanes?

34. It's true that Satan is involved in one way or another with all human sin and suffering, but does that mean he has power to manipulate the gene pool of humans so that he can produce spinal deformities? Is all the suffering in the world his work?

35. What do you make of the curse God brought on the world in response to human rebellion, a curse that he brought on us in order to redeem us? What would be wrong with God's laying all the suffering of the world at our feet and Satan's because he seduced us into sinful rebellion? What if God's holy love brings chastisement and he uses all kinds of secondary agents (natural law, sinful humans, demonic thugs, etc.) to carry out his will?

36. Somebody said that our final and satisfying answer about all the agony in the world is the nature and character of God himself as he has shown himself in Jesus Christ. If you were asked, what would your response be? (See Isaiah 46:3-4.)

BIBLIOGRAPHY

None of what follows is devotional reading, but each of them fully repays the time and energy invested.

Anderson, B. W., ed. *Creation in the Old Testament.* London: SPCK, 1984.

Brueggemann, Walter. *Finally Comes the Poet.* Minneapolis: Fortress Press, 1989.

————. *The Land.* Philadelphia: Fortress Press, 1977.

Davidson, Robertson. *The Courage to Doubt.* London: SCM Press, 1989.

Davies, W. D. *The Gospel and the Land.* Berkeley and Los Angeles: University of California Press, 1974.

Dumbrell, W. J. *Covenant and Creation.* Carlisle, Pa.: Paternoster Press, 1997.

Durham, J. I. *Exodus.* Word Biblical Commentary. Vol. 2. Waco, Tex.: Word, 1987.

Elliot, J. H. *A Home for the Homeless.* Minneapolis: Fortress Press, 1990.

Estes, Steven and Joni Eareckson Tada. *When God Weeps.* Grand Rapids, Mich.: Zondervan, 1997.

Fretheim, T. E. "Because the Whole Earth Is Mine: Theme and Narrative in Exodus." *Interpretation: A Journal of Bible and Theology* 50, no. 3 (July 1996): 229-39.

————. *Exodus.* Interpretation Series. Louisville, Ky.: Knox Press, 1991.

Hicks, John Mark. *Yet Will I Trust Him.* Joplin, Mo.: College Press, 1999.

Josipovici, G. *The Book of God,* 90-107. New Haven, Conn.: Yale University Press, 1990.

Klein, Ralph W. "Back to the Future: The Tabernacle in the Book of Exodus." *Interpretation: A Journal of Bible and Theology* 50, no. 3 (July 1996): 264-76.

Lewis, C. S. *The Screwtape Letters.* San Francisco: HarperSanFrancisco, 2000.

Martens, E. A. *Plot and Purpose in the Old Testament,* 97-115. Leicester, England: InterVarsity, 1981.

O'Donovan, Oliver. *Resurrection and the Moral Order.* Leicester, England: InterVarsity, 1986.

Peters, Ted. *Sin, Radical Evil in Soul and Society.* Grand Rapids, Mich.: Eerdmans, 1994.

Piper, John. *The Pleasures of God.* Portland, Oreg.: Multnomah, 1991.

Plantinga, Cornelius. *Not the Way It's Supposed to Be.* Grand Rapids, Mich.: Eerdmans, 1995.

Ramm, Bernard. *Offense to Reason: The Theology of Sin.* San Francisco: Harper & Row, 1985.

Swartley, W. M. *Israel's Scripture Traditions and the Synoptic Gospels.* Peabody, Mass.: Hendrikson Publishers, 1994.

Thompson, James. *The Church in Exile.* Abilene, Tex.: Abilene Christian University Press, 1990.

VanGemeren, W. A., ed. *New International Dictionary of Old Testament Theology and Exegesis.* 5 vols. Grand Rapids, Mich.: Zondervan, 1997. S.v. "desert."

Westerman, Claus. *Blessing in the Bible and in the Church.* Philadelphia: Fortress Press, 1978.

Notes

Introduction

1. W. M. Clow, *The Cross in the Christian Experience* (London: Hodder & Stoughton, 1908), 51.
2. See 2 Corinthians 10:4-5.

Chapter 2

1. See Psalm 136:5-9 and hear the exultant tone as creation is discussed in Psalm 104.
2. Habakkuk 3:2.
3. 2 Samuel 11:25.
4. Jeremiah 5:24; Matthew 5:45.

Chapter 4

1. Although it is commonly held that babies are born with a "sinful nature," the view is not nearly so common that babies are actually "sinners." To be born with a predisposition to contract cancer is one thing, to have cancer is another. It's widely acknowledged that to be born with a moral/spiritual weakness means we end up actually sinning, and thus becoming sinners is not the same as being born a sinner. Whether we are born with a "sinful nature" is still debated.
2. 2 Thessalonians 1:9.

CHAPTER 6

1. See Luke 24:41.

2. G. K. Chesterton, *The Collected Poems of G. K. Chesterton* (London: Methuon & Co., 1933), 141.

3. See the description of the ark and the tabernacle in Exodus 25:10-22, Exodus 26, and elsewhere.

4. Isaiah 63:9.

5. Hosea 3:2.

CHAPTER 7

1. I've leaned heavily on Frank Boreham for the drift of this section. His piece can be found in *Shadows on the Wall* (London: Epworth), 23-36.

2. See Deuteronomy 25:13-16 as a single illustration from among many.

3. The Viktor Frankl story can be found in his *Man's Search for Meaning* (Boston: Beacon Press, 1966).

CHAPTER 8

1. See Luke 7:23.

CHAPTER 9

1. Abraham Heschel, *The Prophets,* 2 vols. (New York: Harper & Row, 1975). Please see in particular the chapters titled "The Meaning and Mystery of Wrath" and "Ira Dei." All subsequent quotations by Abraham Heschel in this chapter are from the same source.

2. See 1 Peter 4:12-14 and Matthew 5:10-11.

3. Chesterton, *Collected Poems*, 130.

4. See Acts 9:4, Philippians 1:29, and Colossians 1:24.

CHAPTER 10

1. See John 1:45-46 (NKJV, RSV).

CHAPTER 11

1. Take note of a number of connecting verbal links between the words in Psalm 22, the narrative in Judges, and the credo in Deuteronomy 26. For example, the phrase, "They cried out to the Lord for help."

2. See Psalm 73:1-2.

3. See 2 Timothy 1:5; 3:14-15.

4. Note John 11:45 and 12:10-11.

CHAPTER 12

1. See 1 Thessalonians 4:13-18.

CHAPTER 13

1. L. E. Maxwell, *Crowded to Christ* (Chicago: Moody, 1976), 11-12.

CHAPTER 14

1. See 1 Peter 2:21-24; 3:14-18; 4:12-19.

2. The Greek verb *echaristhe* rendered "granted" in Philippians 1:29 has *charis* at its heart, and so the graciousness of the granting is

stressed. The Philippians' suffering on behalf of Christ is a graciously given gift. Have they been graciously given the privilege to believe on him? Even so they have been graciously privileged to suffer on behalf of him.

3. See Acts 9:4 and 1 Peter 4:12-13.

4. P. T. Forsyth, *God the Holy Father* (London: Independent Press, 1957), 33.

5. Robert Browning. The lines are from *Balaustion's Adventure* where Browning (following Euripides, but not too closely) has Heracles laying his life on the line to save Alcestis from death.

CHAPTER 15

1. See Jeremiah 11:19,21; 12:6.

2. Jeremiah 5:1.

3. See Jeremiah 1:6; 4:19-26; 9:1-2; 14:17-19.

4. Shakespeare, *Hamlet,* act 1, scene 5.

5. See Jeremiah 15:10,17; 16:2,5,8.

6. See also Jeremiah 4:10; 12:1; 15:18.

7. Jeremiah 20:8-9.

8. Jeremiah 15:1-2.

9. Jeremiah 18:19-23; 20:12.

10. As quoted in Warren Wiersbe, *Classic Sermons on Hope* (Grand Rapids, Mich.: Kregel, 1994), 47.

CHAPTER 16

1. John Masefield, "The Seekers," in *Poems,* 2 vols. (New York: Macmillan, 1925), 1:124.

2. Robert Louis Stevenson, *Memories and Portraits* (London: Chatto and Windus, 1887), chap. 3, sec. 3.

3. J. S. Stewart, *The River of Life* (Nashville: Abingdon, 1972), 138.

4. William Barclay, *The Letter to the Hebrews,* Daily Study Bible Series (Philadelphia: Westminster, 1957), 170.

5. Walter Brueggemann.

6. As quoted in J. S. Stewart, *The Strong Name* (Edinburgh, 1940), 215-16.

7. "He Who Would Valiant Be," *The Redemption Hymnal,* rev. ed. (London: Oxford University Press, 1955).

CHAPTER 17

1. Paul Scherer, as quoted in *The Interpreter's Bible* (Nashville: Abingdon, 1978), 3:920. I don't go along with all that Scherer and McKechnie say, but I do believe the central thrust of the piece quoted is true and powerful. As it worked out—as God worked it out—Satan makes Job a passionate repudiator of lies about God, a passionate opponent of a caricature of the true God.

CHAPTER 18

1. Bertrand Russel, *Mysticism and Logic* (London: Allen & Unwin, 1951).

2. See Esther 4:1-2.

CHAPTER 19

1. Compare Matthew 16:26.

CHAPTER 20

1. J. B. Priestley, *Literature and Western Man* (London: Readers Union, Heinemann, 1962), 38-39.
2. C. S. Rodd, editorial, *Expository Times* (February 2000).
3. See Hosea 1–2; Isaiah 50:1 and 54:5; Jeremiah 3:14,20.

CHAPTER 21

1. Dan Anders, "Amadeus: When Good Things Happen to Bad People," *Restoration Quarterly* 28, no. 1. I've leaned heavily on his article for the drift of this piece.
2. See 1 Chronicles 16:4-5,37 and the later developments.
3. Psalms 50; 73–83.
4. Jane Stuart Smith and Betty Carlson, *The Gift of Music* (Westchester, Ill.: Crossway, 1988), 54

CHAPTER 22

1. See Job 42:7 and Isaiah 1:11-14.
2. See Revelation 3:14 and 1:16,20.
3. Hebrews 11:16, NASB footnote.
4. See 1 Corinthians 15:10.
5. As translated in *Tanakh: The Holy Scriptures, The New JPS Translation According to the Traditional Hebrew Text* (Philadelphia: Jewish Publication Society, 1988).
6. C. S. Lewis, *The Four Loves* (New York: Harcourt Brace Jovanovich, 1991), chap.: "Charity," quoted in John Piper, *The Pleasures of God* (Portland: Multnomah, 1991), 52.
7. Zephaniah 3:17.

8. Arthur Gossip, *Experience Worketh Hope* (Edinburgh: T&T Clark, 1944), 50-51.

CHAPTER 23

1. See Micah 6:6-8.
2. Mellisat Yesharim, as quoted in Cornelius Platinga, *Not the Way It's Supposed to Be* (Grand Rapids, Mich.: Eerdmans, 1995). This book is an excellent study on sin. You may find it balances the tone of this piece, or maybe this piece brings a bit of balance to his book.
3. See Ezra 9:5-15 and Daniel 9:3-19.
4. Bernard Ramm, regarding Jesus in Matthew 15.
5. Deuteronomy 10:12-13; Romans 13:8-10.

CHAPTER 24

1. C. S. Lewis, *The Screwtape Letters* (London: Centenary Press, 1946), 64-5.
2. Robert Browning, *Pompilia* in *The Ring and the Book*, in *The Poetical Works of Browning*, 2 vols. (London: John Murray, 1915), 2:146-72.

CHAPTER 25

1. Quoted in Frank Boreham, *A Handful of Stars* (London: Epworth Press, 1922), 167-8. The name of the poet is not identified. I've leaned heavily on his piece.
2. See Leviticus 17:11. Scholars strongly agree that the central theme of Leviticus is the presence of God with men, so when it repeatedly

speaks about forgiveness and atonement, we should thankfully acknowledge the link between God's presence and forgiveness.

3. P. T. Forsyth, *Positive Preaching and the Modern Mind* (Grand Rapids, Mich.: Eerdmans, 1966), 37-8.

CHAPTER 26

1. Annie Dillard, *Teaching Stones to Talk* (New York: Harper & Row, 1982), 40.

2. Quoted in William Willimon, *Worship As Pastoral Care* (Nashville: Abingdon, 1986).

3. Willimon, *Pastoral Care*, 63.

4. John Oxenham, quoted in J. G. Lawson, comp., *The Best-Loved Religious Poems* (New York: Revell, 1933), 18.

CHAPTER 27

1. Wilbur Rees, *$3.00 Worth of God* (Valley Forge, Pa.: Judson Press, 1971), 43.

2. Jacob Neusner, *An Introduction to Judaism* (Louisville, Ky.: Westminster/John Knox Press, 1991), 54.

3. See Isaiah 46:3-4.

CHAPTER 28

1. Irving Bacheller, *Eben Holden* (Boston: Lothrop, 1903).

2. Compare 1 Corinthians 2:9.

3. Robert Browning, "Rabbi Ben Ezra" in *The Poetical Works of Robert Browning*, 2 vols. (London: Wordsworth, 1915), 1:580.

Printed in the United States
by Baker & Taylor Publisher Services